More Lake District

WALKS

Compiled by
Brian Conduit
and John Watney

JARROLD

Acknowledgements
We would like to thank Mrs Ruth Evans, Mrs Lynn Wilson,
Mr Arthur Williams and staff from the Lake District National
Park, Cumbria County Council, and the many tourist informa-
tion offices in the area for their valuable advice and assistance
as well as Mr Tony Iles, Mr Jo Leighton and Mr David
Woodhead for their help in updating the information on
several routes.

Text:	Brian Conduit and John Watney
Photography:	Jarrold Publishing, John Watney, Bill Birkett
Editor:	Geoffrey Sutton
Designers:	Brian Skinner, Doug Whitworth

Series Consultant: Brian Conduit

Jarrold Publishing   ISBN 0-7117-0817-7

While every care has been taken to ensure the accuracy of the
route directions, the publishers cannot accept responsibility
for errors or omissions, or for changes in details given. The
countryside is not static: hedges and fences can be removed,
field boundaries can be altered, footpaths can be rerouted and
changes in ownership can result in the closure or diversion of
some concessionary paths. Also, paths that are easy and
pleasant for walking in fine conditions may become slippery,
muddy and difficult in wet weather, while stepping-stones
across rivers and streams may become impassable.

If you find an inaccuracy in either the text or maps, please
write or e-mail to Jarrold Publishing at the address below.

First published 1995
by Jarrold Publishing and Ordnance Survey
Revised reprints 1997 and 2001

Printed in Belgium
by Proost NV, Turnhout. 3/01

Jarrold Publishing
Pathfinder Guides, Whitefriars, Norwich NR3 1TR
E-mail: pathfinder@jarrold.com
www.jarrold-publishing.co.uk/pathfinders

Front cover:	Spout Head, on the corridor route from Scafell Pike
Previous page:	Remains of the station and Nab Gill Mine at Boot

Contents

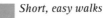 *Short, easy walks*

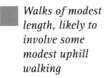 *Walks of modest
length, likely to
involve some
modest uphill
walking*

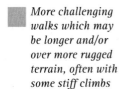 *More challenging
walks which may
be longer and/or
over more rugged
terrain, often with
some stiff climbs*

Keymap 1

Keymap 2

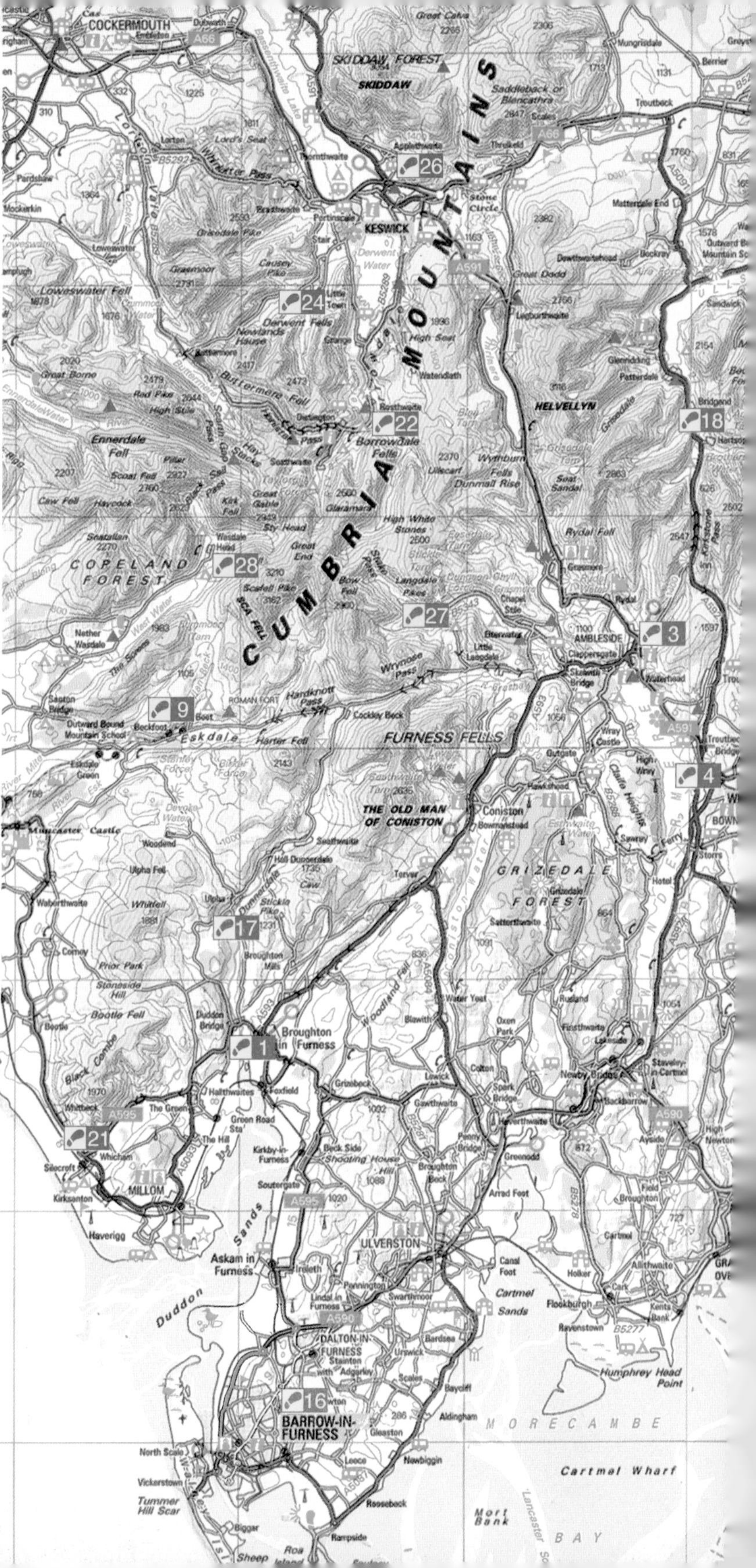

COCKERMOUTH
SKIDDAW FOREST
SKIDDAW
CUMBRIAN MOUNTAINS
Saddleback or Blencathra
KESWICK
Derwent Water
Lorton
Whinlatter Pass
Grasmoor
Causey Pike
Loweswater Fell
Derwent Fells
Newlands Hause
Great Borne
Buttermere Fell
Red Pike
High Stile
Ennerdale Fell
Borrowdale Fells
HELVELLYN
Great Dodd
High Seat
Watendlath
Rosthwaite
Pillar
Scoat Fell
Haycock
Caw Fell
Great Gable
Glaramara
Sty Head
Kirk Fell
High White Stones
Ullscarf
Wythburn Fells
Dunmail Rise
Seat Sandal
Rydal Fell
Grasmere
COPELAND FOREST
Great End
Scafell Pike
Bow Fell
Langdale Pikes
Scafell
Wasdale Head
Nether Wasdale
The Screes
Wast Water
AMBLESIDE
Clappersgate
Rydal
Waterhead
Little Langdale
Wrynose Pass
Hardknott Pass
ROMAN FORT
Cockley Beck
FURNESS FELLS
Eskdale
Harter Fell
Boot
Beckfoot
Outward Bound Mountain School
Eskdale Green
Birker Force
Stanley Force
River Mite
River Esk
Devoke Water
Muncaster Castle
Woodend
Ulpha Fell
Whitfell
Waberthwaite
THE OLD MAN OF CONISTON
Coniston
Hawkshead
Esthwaite Water
GRIZEDALE FOREST
Grizedale
Satterthwaite
Torver
Coniston Water
Hall Dunnerdale
Stickle Pike
Ulpha
Broughton Mills
Corney
Prior Park
Stoneside Hill
Bootle Fell
Bootle
Black Combe
Duddon Bridge
Broughton in Furness
Woodland Fell
Water Yeat
Blawith
Oxen Park
Rusland
Finsthwaite
Lakeside
Newby Bridge
Staveley-in-Cartmel
Backbarrow
Annaside
Whitbeck
The Green
Hallthwaites
Foxfield
Grizebeck
Lowick
Colton
Spark Bridge
Gawthwaite
Green Road Sta
The Hill
Whicham
Silecroft
MILLOM
Kirksanton
Haverigg
Kirkby-in-Furness
Beck Side
Shooting House Hill
Penny Bridge
Greenodd
Haverthwaite
Broughton Beck
Arrad Foot
Soutergate
Duddon Sands
Askam in Furness
Ireleth
ULVERSTON
Pennington
Swarthmoor
Lindal in Furness
Canal Foot
Cartmel Sands
Holker
Cark
Flookburgh
Ravenstown
Allithwaite
Kents Bank
Cartmel
Field Broughton
Ayside
DALTON-IN-FURNESS
Stainton with Adgarley
Urswick
Bardsea
Scales
Baycliff
Aldingham
Humphrey Head Point
MORECAMBE
BARROW-IN-FURNESS
Gleaston
North Scale
Vickerstown
Tummer Hill Scar
Leece
Newbiggin
Roosebeck
Rampside
Biggar
Sheep
Cartmel Wharf
Mort Bank
BAY
Lancaster
Wray Castle
High Wray
Claife Heights
Sawrey
Ferry
Storrs
Troutbeck
Mungrisdale
Threlkeld
Applethwaite
Braithwaite
Portinscale
Thornthwaite
Lord's Seat
Grange
Little Town
Buttermere
Seathwaite
Stone Circle
Legburthwaite
Thirlmere
Glenridding
Patterdale
Grisedale
Matterdale End
Dockray
Bridgend
Kirkstone Pass
Troutbeck Bridge
A66
A591
A5091
A593
A595
A590
A5092
B5292
B5289
B5343
B5285
B5278
B5277
A5087

SCALE 1:294 118 or 1 INCH to about 4¾ MILES *1CM to 2.9KM*

0   2   4   6   8   10   KILOMETRES   15

0   2   4   6   MILES   8   10

KEYMAP HEIGHTS SHOWN IN FEET

Walk	Page	Start	Nat. Grid Reference	Distance	Time	Highest Point
Angle Tarn and Hayeswater	58	Brothers Water	NY 403133	7 miles (11.3km)	3½ hrs	1706ft (520m)
Arnside Knott and Tower	38	Arnside	SD 453786	6 miles (9.7km)	3 hrs	98ft (30m)
Black Combe	66	Silecroft	SD 131822	5½ miles (8.9km)	3 hrs	1970ft (600m)
Broughton in Furness	14	Broughton in Furness	SD 212875	3 miles (4.8km)	1½ hrs	131ft (40m)
Boot	32	Boot	NY 173007	4¼ miles (6.8km)	2¼ hrs	656ft (200m)
Carrock Fell and High Pike	71	Calebreck	NY 350350	7¼ miles (11.7km)	3¾ hrs	2174ft (663m)
Cockermouth and the Derwent valley	40	Cockermouth	NY 118309	7½ miles (12.1km)	3 hrs	705ft (215m)
Cross Fell	76	Kirkland	NY 650325	8½ miles (13.7km)	5 hrs	2930ft (893m)
Dunnerdale Fells	56	Ulpha Bridge	SD 198920	6½ miles (10.5km)	3½ hrs	820ft (250m)
Eden, Beside the River	16	Great Corby	NY 471545	3 miles (4.8km)	1¾ hrs	98ft (30m)
Hadrian's Wall and the River Irthing	47	Birdoswald	NY 616664	7½ miles (12.1km)	3½ hrs	525ft (160m)
Hesket Newmarket and Caldbeck	28	Hesket Newmarket	NY 341386	5 miles (8km)	2½ hrs	623ft (190m)
Kendal, Scout Scar and Cunswick Fell	44	Kendal	SD 514925	7 miles (11.3km)	3½ hrs	689ft (210m)
Kentmere valley	30	Kentmere	NY 456041	6½ miles (10.5km)	3½ hrs	853ft (260m)
Lacy's Caves and Long Meg and her Daughters	22	Little Salkeld	NY 565362	5 miles (8km)	2½ hrs	590ft (180m)
Langdale Pikes	83	New Dungeon Ghyll Hotel	NY 294064	9 miles (14.5km)	6½ hrs	2000ft (610m)
Low and High Sweden bridges	18	Ambleside	NY 376045	3½ miles (5.6km)	2 hrs	656ft (200m)
Low Furness	52	Furness Abbey	SD 218716	7½ miles (12.1km)	3½ hrs	262ft (80m)
Lowther, River, and Shap Abbey	60	Shap	NY 563150	5½ miles (8.9km)	3 hrs	951ft (290m)
Mallerstang and Pendragon Castle	63	Aisgill Moor Cottages	SD 777963	9 miles (14.5km)	4½ hrs	1410ft (430m)
Newlands Horseshoe	74	Little Town	NY 231193	8½ miles (13.7km)	5½ hrs	2473ft (753m)
Orrest Head	20	Windermere	SD 412987	3 miles (4.8km)	1½ hrs	784ft (238m)
Rosthwaite, Watendlath and Stonethwaite	68	Rosthwaite	NY 257147	5 miles (8km)	4 hrs	1444ft (440m)
St Bees Head	35	St Bees seafront	NX 960117	6½ miles (10.5km)	4 hrs	800ft (240m)
Scafell Pike	86	Wasdale Head	NY 186083	8 miles (12.9km)	7 hrs	3210ft (978m)
Skiddaw	80	Latrigg, Keswick	NY 281253	8 miles (12.9km)	5 hrs	3053ft (931m)
Solway coast	25	Port Carlisle	NY 240622	6 miles (9.7km)	4 hrs	66ft (20m)
Ullswater	50	Pooley Bridge	NY 469244	6½ miles (10.5km)	3¼ hrs	1000ft (305m)

Comments

Impressive views over Ullswater, Brothers Water and the surrounding fells can be enjoyed from the higher points on the walk.

Plenty of variety on a walk that includes a superb viewpoint, attractive woodland, a ruined tower, cliffs, coastal marshes and an estuary.

A relatively easy 'there and back' walk to the summit of Black Combe, which gives superb views both inland and along the Cumbrian coast.

A short and relaxing walk that gives fine views of the Dunnerdale Fells and Black Combe.

The Esk valley is one of the Lake District's loveliest, and this walk passes waterfalls and a tarn to reach moorland overlooking Sca Fell and Great Gable.

Having climbed the rock- and scree-strewn slopes, you see the great expanse of the Vale of Eden lying at your feet.

This walk follows a section of the Allerdale Ramble, crosses the River Derwent at Isel Bridge and then runs back to Cockermouth.

This is a walk for good weather, when the effort to gain the highest point on the Pennines is rewarded with a vast panoramic view – even unto Scotland.

At the end of this walk you may well agree with Wordsworth that the Duddon is the loveliest of rivers.

This short stretch of the River Eden offers the walker many grand views and interesting sites, especially enjoyable in midsummer.

See evidence of the Roman occupation in the form of a milecastle, a fort and a section of wall as well as a gorge cleft by the River Irthing, which formed a natural defence.

John Peel knew the two villages that link this walk, and would have enjoyed the splendid views as he hunted over the surrounding fells.

From the limestone escarpment of Scout Scar, there are superb views looking across to the Lakeland mountains.

An easy walk that takes you up and down the narrow Kentmere valley, hemmed in by steep, lonely and impressive fells.

Sandstone caves overhanging the River Eden, a section of the Carlisle–Settle railway and a stone henge are all encompassed in this short walk.

There are no easy routes to attain the tops of these volcanic crags, but at 2000 feet (610m) they peer down into the heart of south-west Lakeland.

From Ambleside the route heads up and down the valley of Scandale Beck, giving grand views of the head of Windermere.

From the extensive and well-preserved ruins of Furness Abbey, this walk explores part of the Furness peninsula to the south of the Lake District.

This walk, on the eastern edge of the Lake District, provides views across empty moorland and passes by the ruins of a medieval abbey.

Cumbria and the River Eden are at their remotest between Wild Boar Fell and Mallerstang Edge, which is the highest point on the Carlisle–Settle line.

From this grand ridge walk around the Newlands valley, a Lake District classic, you enjoy a succession of magnificent and constantly changing views.

Although a relatively modest hill, the views from Orrest Head, especially over Windermere, are outstanding.

This is Borrowdale at its most dramatic: remote hamlets, towering fells, high tarns and a noted wetland.

The clifftops, home to nesting seabirds, give a grandstand view to Galloway, the Isle of Man and the Mourne Mountains.

England's highest peak is a magnet for walkers and offers incomparable views in good weather, but it is no place for the inexperienced.

Skiddaw's formidable massif, which dominates the north-west of the county, is popular with walkers, who can opt to return by the easier outward route.

A level walk that embraces a wealth of interest: bogland plants, mudflats, port and canal remains, an RSPB reserve and the site of the most westerly fort on Hadrian's Wall.

Whether walking along its shore or gazing down on it from the crags of Barton Fell, Ullswater is always a lovely sight.

At-a-glance...

Introduction to the Lake District

In this second title on the Lake District in the pathfinder series, a number of walks have been included that are either on the periphery of or outside the boundaries of the national park. There are two main reasons for this: the first is to reduce some of the pressure on the more popular parts of the Lake District, and the second is to encourage walkers to visit other areas of Cumbria where there is much superb and varied scenery. Therefore, as well as walks in the familiar and much-loved landscapes of mountains and lakes, this selection includes others that embrace stretches of the Cumbrian coast from Morecambe Bay to the Solway Firth, the Furness peninsula, the western parts of Hadrian's Wall, the Eden valley and the Cumbrian Pennines. All these areas offer enjoyable walking and can easily be combined with a visit to the Lake District itself.

Friendly and Welcoming Grandeur

This delectable landscape of lakes and mountains, valleys and waterfalls has captivated and enchanted millions of visitors but, at the same time, its unique scenic beauty is somewhat difficult to analyse. For after all, even within this small island there are other lake and mountain areas which have higher mountains and larger lakes – not that grandeur, beauty or even ruggedness are dependent upon size alone. Perhaps this is where the clue to the uniqueness of the Lake District lies. All the essential ingredients of a mountain landscape are there, but on a comparatively small scale, so that its grandeur seems friendly and welcoming rather than forbidding. From almost all the major peaks you look down on peaceful, green, wooded valleys, which have a lushness you might associate with gentler landscapes further south, and these are dotted with attractive villages, whose pubs and tearooms are a mecca for weary ramblers coming down from the fells.

Geological Roots

The physical features of Lakeland are inevitably rooted in its geology. In simple terms there are three broad, roughly parallel bands of rock extending across the area from west to east. Oldest of these are the Skiddaw slates in the north which, though hard, have been eroded by weather over a long period of time to produce a landscape of relatively smooth and rounded hills, such as Blencathra and Skiddaw itself. Next comes the central zone of volcanic rocks, sometimes called the Borrowdale Series, which are highly weather-resistant. These have given rise to the craggy outline of the 'central massif', including Sca Fell, Great Gable, the Langdale Pikes, Coniston Old Man and Helvellyn. Lastly come the softer

Silurian rocks of the southern band, the youngest rocks, stretching from Coniston Water across to Windermere and Kendal, and creating a gentler landscape than further north. Around the edges of these main bands are areas of limestone and sandstone and the coal measures that gave rise to the west coast industrial area around Workington and Whitehaven, and also outcrops of granite in Eskdale and elsewhere.

Stickle Tarn and Harrison Stickle, Langdale Pikes

The Ice Age had the most striking effect on the landscape of the Lake District. As the glaciers moved outwards from the central fells, they scoured out and rounded the main valleys into their present U-shapes, leaving tributary 'hanging valleys' stranded high up on the sides, from which water cascades down in spectacular falls. At the same time, the glaciers also gouged out the depressions into which the lakes and tarns were formed and restricted their outlets by depositing debris called moraines. In some cases, the build-up of these moraines caused a single lake to be divided into two smaller ones, clearly seen at Keswick.

Celts, Romans, Angles and Norsemen

With its damp climate, rugged terrain and comparatively thin soils, the Lake District was not one of the main centres of population in prehistoric Britain, but there are some monuments of this period, principally the spectacular Bronze Age stone circle at Castlerigg, near Keswick. The interest of the Romans in the area was purely military, and the Cumbrian coast became a logical extension of Hadrian's Wall, with a line of forts stretching along it. Chief of these was Ravenglass. From here the Romans drove a road through the heart of the Lake District, via the Hardknott and Wrynose passes, to the fort at Ambleside and thence along the High Street ridge, the line of which is now a magnificent footpath, to link up with their fort near Brougham. Along this route are remains which show not only the military power of the Romans but also their standards of comfort and hygiene, notably the Bath House at Ravenglass and the dramatically sited Hardknott Fort, which commands the head of Eskdale.

The collapse of Roman power was followed by several centuries of confusion, in which native Celts and successive waves of invaders, first Angles, and later Norsemen, struggled for supremacy. In its relative isolation, protected by natural mountain defences, the Lake District was one of the areas where, for a time, the Celts were able to resist the penetration of the Angles from the south and east, maintaining the independent kingdom of Strathclyde, which straddled the present English-Scottish border. The name 'Cumbria' in fact comes from the Celtic *cymry* meaning 'comrades' – the Welsh word for the Welsh.

More successful invaders were the Norsemen, who moved into the area from the coast, coming via Ireland and the Isle of Man, and developed small farming communities in the remote western valleys. Norse influence on the region is still strong: in the common place-name ending -thwaite, in the use of Norse words to describe physical features – gill, beck, tarn and force – and in the Viking crosses at Gosforth and elsewhere.

Frontier Region

For centuries Cumbria was a debatable frontier region, claimed by both English and Scottish kings. This was why William the Conqueror did not include it in his 'Domesday' survey in 1086, and it was not until after his son, William II, captured Carlisle in 1092 and established a strong royal fortress there that the border was finally fixed.

Following the Norman Conquest came the monastic orders, who also established their sites around the edge of, rather than within, the Lake District, at Holme Cultram, St Bees, Calder, Cartmel, Shap and Lanercost. These monasteries owned considerable land and played a major role in the economic development of the region: clearing woods, extending sheep-farming and exploiting minerals, principally the iron ores of Furness.

Drystone Walls

Agricultural prosperity came later to the Lake District than to most other parts of England but, when it did, in the late 17th century, it produced the same great rebuilding of farmhouses as elsewhere, and some fine examples exist of yeoman farmers' or statesmen's houses of the period, such as Town End, near Troutbeck. During the late 18th and early 19th centuries came the enclosure movement, when miles of drystone walls spread from the valleys onto the open fells.

Sheep, Quarries and Mines

Industrial activity in the area was at its height from the late 16th to the 19th century, especially woollen cloth manufacturing around Kendal and Hawkshead, the quarrying of granite and slate, and the mining of copper in Borrowdale and around Coniston, iron ore in Furness, and graphite ('wad' or 'plumbago') in Borrowdale, which gave rise to Keswick's famous pencil industry. Although the scars from these industries are gradually disappearing, they still provide a fascinating field for archaeologists. The most popular survival of Eskdale's granite-quarrying industry, however, is the narrow-gauge Ravenglass and Eskdale Railway, now a superb tourist attraction.

From Poetry to Tourism

Despite these developments, the Lake District remained a relatively little-known backwater until towards the end of the 18th century, when the first tourists started to arrive. Lakeland tourism was largely initiated by William Wordsworth and the other Lake Poets, who were among the foremost leaders of the Romantic movement, when there was an awakening interest in the wilder areas of Britain, previously shunned as being both barbaric and dangerous. Wordsworth is the greatest of all the many Lakeland literary figures and, unlike some of the others, was a native Cumbrian. Born at Cockermouth and educated at Hawkshead, he lived most of his life in the Lake District, especially around Grasmere and Rydal. Once his fame was established, he attracted a group of poets around him – Robert Southey, Samuel Taylor Coleridge and Thomas De Quincey, known collectively as the 'Lake Poets', and since their time a series of other varied literary figures have flocked into the Lake District to make temporary or permanent homes there, including Sir Walter Scott, Lord Tennyson, John Ruskin, Arthur Ransome, Beatrix Potter and Sir Hugh Walpole.

Birthplace of Conservation

Tourism, large-scale quarrying and, later on, demands for reservoirs and forestry in the Lake District brought forth the conservationist movements, many of which originated in the area. The Lake District Defence Society, forerunner of the Friends of the Lake District, was founded in 1883. Canon Rawnsley, Vicar of Crosthwaite, near Keswick, was one of the founders and main driving forces behind the National Trust (founded in 1895), whose earliest properties were acquired in the Lakes at Brandelhow, on the western side of Derwent Water, and Gowbarrow on the shores of Ullswater (where Wordsworth is alleged to have seen the daffodils that inspired the best-known poem in the English language). The National Trust now owns about 25 per cent of the area.

Largest National Park

The designation of the Lake District as a national park in 1951, the largest in area of Britain's ten national parks, was a conservation victory. Although this is England's only mountain region, the Lake District is not a walking area just for super-fit fell-walkers. Along with tough ascents, there are plenty of middle- and lower-level walks, from which the views are just as varied and spectacular, and easy, attractive circuits of several of the lakes are possible, which make excellent half-day walks.

Walking in the Lake District is a pastime that can be enjoyed by people of all ages, all degrees of fitness and all interests. The Lake District is truly, as Wordsworth said, anticipating the later creation of the national park, 'a sort of national property, in which every man has a right and an interest who has an eye to perceive and a heart to enjoy'.

Broughton in Furness

Start	Broughton in Furness
Distance	3 miles (4.8km)
Approximate time	1½ hours
Parking	Around the Square at Broughton in Furness
Refreshments	Pubs and cafés at Broughton in Furness
Ordnance Survey maps	Landranger 96 (Barrow-in-Furness & South Lakeland), Outdoor Leisure 6 (The English Lakes – South Western area)

This short and easy walk explores the pleasant countryside around Broughton in Furness just to the north of the Duddon Sands. There are some splendid views of the Dunnerdale Fells and across the Duddon estuary to the bulk of Black Combe. Some paths may be muddy after heavy rain.

A dignified, tree-shaded Georgian square is a rarity in this fairly remote part of Cumbria and it gives the small town of Broughton in Furness something of the flavour and appearance of a French provincial town. On one side of the Square is the late 18th-century town hall, now a tourist information centre. The church, which stands some distance away, has been enlarged and rebuilt several times, the last occasion being in the late 19th century, but retains a fine Norman doorway from the original building.

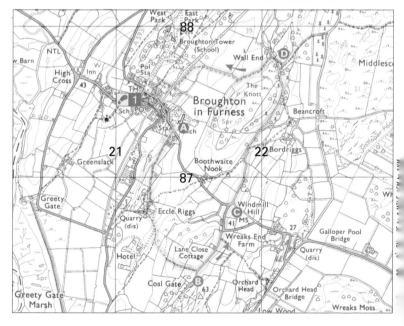

Looking over Broughton in Furness to the Duddon valley

Start in the Square, walk down Market Street, keep ahead and follow the road uphill around right and left bends. At a Cumbria Coastal Way sign opposite a school entrance, turn right along an enclosed, walled tarmac track **Ⓐ**.

From this track there are fine views to the right over Broughton, the Duddon valley and estuary, and Black Combe. After passing to the left of a house, the track becomes hedge-lined and heads downhill, continuing past cottages to a footpath sign on the edge of trees. Bear left through the trees, go through a metal kissing-gate and then half-left downhill across a golf-course. Cross a plank footbridge (Cumbria Way), keep ahead to cross a more substantial footbridge over a stream, bear right towards a gateway where a Cumbria Coastal Way footpath sign shows the position of a stone stile. Climb it, head uphill along the right-hand edge of a field, by a wall on the right, go through a metal gate in the wall and continue along the left-hand edge of a field. Go through another metal gate, continue first along a walled path and then by a wall on the right, and go through a metal gate on to a tarmac track **Ⓑ**.

Turn left along the track to a road, continue along it and, at a sharp left-hand bend, keep ahead **Ⓒ** along a hedge-lined tarmac track. Follow this track for ³/₄ mile (1.2km) entering attractive woodland, and, just before reaching Wall End Farm, turn left over a stile, at a public footpath sign **Ⓓ**. Head up an embankment and at the top continue across a sloping meadow, veering right to walk along its bottom edge, by a wall on the right. After a slight descent, look out for and turn right over a squeezer stile, continue along the right-hand edge of a field, by a wall on the right, and go through another squeezer stile in the field corner.

Continue along the right-hand edge of the next narrow field, turn left in the corner to continue along the field edge, by a wire fence bordering trees on the right, pass between gateposts and keep ahead to go through a gap in the corner of the next field. Turn right over a stone stile, cross a track and keep ahead along the track, round to the left to return to the Square. ●

Beside the River Eden

Start	Great Corby
Distance	3 miles (4.8km)
Approximate time	1¾ hours
Parking	On wide part of road by Great Corby
Refreshments	Pub at Great Corby, pubs, hotels and restaurant at Wetheral
Ordnance Survey maps	Landranger 86 (Haltwhistle, Bewcastle & Alston area), Pathfinder 558, NY 45/55 (Carlisle (East) & Castle Carrock)

This is an easy walk along one of the more scenic reaches of the River Eden, not far from Carlisle, and takes in a remarkable number of views and sites of interest for such a short distance. The best lighting for the river scenery is in the afternoon and particularly a midsummer early evening.

Start by walking northwards to the level-crossing **A** and turn left onto the wooden footpath on the downstream side of the railway viaduct that leads to the station at Wetheral on the far bank. Here there is a spectacular view down the Eden. Cross to the opposite platform by the footbridge and leave the station yard **B** down a steep path with steps made out of old railway sleepers. The way turns under the viaduct to the water's edge, where you turn upstream along Low Road, which rises a little above the river. At a T-junction with a lane from the village, turn left and go down a few steps onto a grass bank beside the water **C**. Follow a signposted grassy path to a kissing-gate at the entrance to Wetheral Woods **D**.

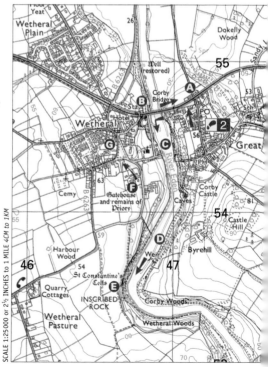

SCALE 1:25000 or 2½ INCHES to 1 MILE 4CM to 1KM

From the riverside you can see a series of caves, carved out of the red sandstone of the escarpment below Corby Castle, and an architectural oddity – a statue of Nelson above a flight of steps leading down to the water. Behind him, when there has been plenty of rain, a cascade pours down the rock face from the mouths of two mythical creatures, but binoculars are needed to see all the details. In several places on this section of the walk, flat rocks in the river can be used as stepping-stones to get views downstream of Corby Castle, which originally dates from the 14th century but is now mostly a Georgian mansion. It makes a fine sight, perched 90 feet (27.5m) above a slight bend in the river.

Corby Castle caves above the River Eden, otherwise known as Wetheral Safeguards

Keep on the path through Wetheral Woods, which climbs above the riverbank, and look out for a gap in the trees and a way down to the water from which you can see ancient fish traps and a salmon leap, built by the medieval monks of Wetheral Priory, on the opposite shore. At the far end of the woods there is a great sequoia, or coast redwood, one of the tallest species of tree in the world. There are several paths, but at each junction keep to the left until you reach a ledge overhanging the water that takes you to three square-cut caves **E**. These are St Constantine's Cells or Wetheral Safeguards; the link with St Constantine is tenuous and the alternative name is more realistic, referring to the local monks who used them to store valuables.

From the cells, go back a short distance to a set of six steps on the left that lead up to a higher path. Turn right along it, climb a stile into a field and follow a line of oaks to a gate onto a lane. The lane leads downhill into Wetheral, and on the way you pass the gatehouse of Wetheral Priory **F**. The priory was founded in 1088, and this is all that remains of it, apart from a few fragments of wall in the buildings of Wetheral Priory Farm.

The lane enters the village by the church, built in the Early English style with a Victorian tower. Walk uphill away from the river into the village. Take either the road along the top or the bottom of the lovely triangular green **G** and at the far end take the lane to the right down to the station. Go over the footbridge and back across the viaduct to return to the start.

Low and High Sweden bridges

Start	Ambleside
Distance	3½ miles (5.6km)
Approximate time	2 hours
Parking	Ambleside
Refreshments	Pubs and cafés at Ambleside
Ordnance Survey maps	Landranger 90 (Penrith, Keswick & Ambleside), Outdoor Leisure 7 (The English Lakes – South Eastern area)

This short and easy route, ideal for a leisurely afternoon stroll, heads up out of Ambleside to Low Sweden Bridge and then climbs steadily above the valley of Scandale Beck before descending to the picturesque High Sweden Bridge. Initially, the return section passes through attractive woodland beside the beck, and on the final stretch there are impressive views over the surrounding fells and the head of Windermere.

Situated on a main road at the head of Windermere, Ambleside has developed into one of the Lake District's major tourist centres. Although a visitor might come away with the overriding impression of a 19th-century town, the period when most of its hotels and guest houses were built, Ambleside is not just a creation of the Victorian tourist era; the Romans built their fort of Galava here, an important centre for their communications network in north-west England. At the far end of the town stands what is undoubtedly Ambleside's most photographed building: the tiny 17th-century Bridge House, built above the bridge over Stock Ghyll and now a National Trust Information Centre.

Start by the cross, Market Hall and Queen's Hotel and walk along North Road. At a junction, turn left down Smithy Brow

Ambleside and the head of Windermere

and take the first turning on the right, Nook Lane. Follow this narrow tarmac lane gently uphill, passing to the right of the buildings of Charlotte Mason College (part of the University of Lancaster) and, after passing between farm buildings, continue along a rough track.

Turn left over Low Sweden Bridge **A** – to the right are some impressive wooded falls – and continue along the track, which bends sharply to the right. Head steadily and unrelentingly uphill above the wooded valley on the right, follow the track around left and right bends and continue uphill, by a wall on the left, passing through several wall gaps to the left of what are now redundant ladder-stiles. At a fork, take the right-hand track, pass through another wall gap to the left of a ladder-stile, continue ahead for another 50 yds (46m), passing a sheepfold on the right, and then turn right **B** along an obvious grassy path between bracken down to a ladder-stile.

Climb the stile and continue downhill, by a wall on the left, to cross High Sweden Bridge **C**, an old pack-horse bridge in a beautiful setting. Now follow an attractive wooded path beside the rocky waters of Scandale Beck to a gate. Go through, continue through the woodland of Rough Sides, go through another gate and walk along a walled track, soon emerging from the trees.

After a brief, gentle climb to leave the beck, you

continue along an enclosed track gently downhill, enjoying the grand views to the right of Rydal Water and particularly impressive views ahead of Ambleside and the head of Windermere. Go through a gate, continue downhill along a tarmac lane into Ambleside, turn right at a T-junction and bear left along North Road to return to the start. ●

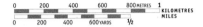

Orrest Head

Start	Windermere
Distance	3 miles (4.8km)
Approximate time	1½ hours
Parking	Layby on A591 near Windermere station and Tourist Information Centre
Refreshments	Pubs and cafés at Windermere
Ordnance Survey maps	Landranger 96 (Barrow-in-Furness & South Lakeland), Outdoor Leisure 7 (The English Lakes – South Eastern area)

Many fellwalkers, including Wainwright, have first 'cut their teeth' on Orrest Head, a hill to the north of Windermere Town that, despite rising to a modest height of only 784ft (238m), gives outstanding views up and down the length of Windermere and across to the central fells. The walk first passes through pleasant woodland at the base of the hill before heading up to the summit, an easy and gradual climb, which is then followed by an equally easy descent.

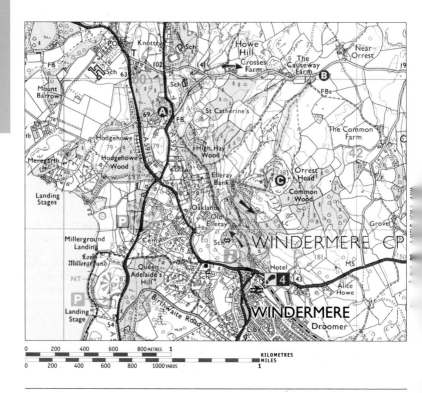

Windermere, north from Orrest Head

It was the coming of the railway in 1847 that led to the development of Windermere, previously a small village called Braithwaite. Over the following years many hotels and guest-houses sprang up to cater for the visitors that flocked into the area, and as a result the 'new town' by the rail terminal became virtually continuous with the older lakeside resort of Bowness.

The walk starts at the Tourist Information Centre. Cross the A591, turn left for a few yards and, at a footpath sign to Orrest Head, turn right onto a tarmac track. After a few yards, bear left off it, at a public footpath sign 'A592 Troutbeck Road', along a track through woodland, by a wall on the left. Descend slightly to pass to the right of a house and continue along the narrow path opposite, by an iron fence on your left side.

At a tarmac drive, turn right for a few yards and in front of the gate to Ellery Bank, continue along a path to the left of the gateposts, still by an iron fence on the left, through more attractive woodland. Descend gently to cross a footbridge, go through a metal gate, follow a path across a field, cross a track and keep ahead to go through a metal gate onto a road **Ⓐ**. Immediately turn right onto a lane and follow this pleasant, winding lane –

initially uphill, later it levels off – for nearly ³⁄₄ mile (1.2km). Ignore the first public footpath sign to the right but at the second one climb a stone stile in the wall on the right **Ⓑ**.

Continue along a path by a wall on the right and, where the wall veers to the right, keep straight ahead, climbing steadily across grass and between rocky outcrops. Later bear right to rejoin the wall, climb a stone stile in the wall corner and continue between bracken up to the 784ft (238m) summit of Orrest Head **Ⓒ**, marked by benches and a view indicator. The view here is magnificent: up and down the whole length of Windermere and across to the array of peaks of southern Lakeland, the line of the Pennines and Morecambe Bay.

From the summit, bear slightly right along a path that descends to a metal kissing-gate in a wall corner. Go through it, turn right along a tree-lined path, between a wire fence on the left and a wall on the right, and continue along the right, inside edge of sloping woodland. At a white arrow post, turn left to continue through trees and, where the rough path ends, keep ahead along a narrow, tarmac track.

Follow the track downhill through woodland and around several sharp bends back to your starting point at Windermere.

Lacy's Caves and Long Meg and her Daughters

Start	Little Salkeld
Distance	5 miles (8km)
Approximate time	2½ hours
Parking	Roadside parking at Little Salkeld
Refreshments	None
Ordnance Survey maps	Landranger 90 (Penrith, Keswick & Ambleside), Pathfinder 577, NY 43/53 (Penrith (North))

Lying between two quiet sandstone villages in the Eden valley, this walk takes in part of the Settle–Carlisle line, with the chance of seeing steam locomotives, an 18th-century folly, carved out of the cliffs overhanging the River Eden, and a stone henge second in importance only to Stonehenge itself. There are near views of the north Pennines, and more distant ones of the eastern fells of the Lake District.

Little Salkeld, where the walk starts, derives from the Norse for 'the spring among the willows'. Park on one of the roads off the village green and take the right-hand fork **Ⓐ** at the end of the wall around Salkeld Hall (not open to the public) onto a farm road marked 'Public Footpath only'. This road runs beside the railway line. On the way it passes through the sidings that served the nearby Long Meg gypsum and anhydrite mines, remains of which are clearly visible. The products made plaster of Paris and sulphuric acid respectively.

At a notice 'Private Long Meg', turn sharp left down a track, sign-posted 'Lacy's Caves and Daleraven' beside an electricity substation **Ⓑ**. Keep between wire fences next to the sidings and go into the woods opposite a 60ft- (18m) high viaduct that carries the railway over the river. Shortly after passing a weir on the left, look out for an indistinct little path

that goes a few yards down to the riverbank and the remains of a turbine house **Ⓒ**, which once produced electricity for the mine. This can be slippery after rain, and great care must be taken, especially with children.

The path now runs through Cave Wood, along a ledge above meadows on one side and a rock escarpment on the other. It is in fact the bed of the former mine tramway, and here and there it is possible to trip up on half-buried bits of permanent way. On the right of the path are vestiges of inclined planes and loading bays. The trees of the wood are beech and oak with a ground-cover of balsam and butterbur. Where the path starts up a small riverside cliff, take another narrow path to the left, which leads round the cliff-face to Lacy's Caves. A narrow ledge runs in front of the five caves, with a sheer drop to the river, but they are interconnected and can be visited in succession with complete safety. Crudely pointed, arched entrances and 'windows' give them a Gothic look, with traces of a cultivated garden around them. They were hewn out of the soft red sandstone for the eccentric Colonel Samuel Lacy, the owner of Salkeld Hall, in about 1867. There are many stories about them, but it seems most likely that he used them for summer parties or somewhere to sit and enjoy views of the river.

The route continues on from the caves through a plantation of Norway spruce and then along the bottom of a flowery meadow, sloping down to the river, to Daleraven Bridge **D** on the Glassonby–Kirkoswald road. Turn right on the road and walk about ½ mile (800m) uphill to Glassonby. As you go, the Pennines, including Cross Fell, their highest point, loom ahead. Glassonby is small with no shop or pub, but it does have a smithy. Keep to the right, past the tiny village green, and follow the road signposted to Little Salkeld, past Glassonby Hall (a house with an enclosed courtyard) and, beyond another house, turn right at a stone barn **E** up the lane to Addingham's Church of St Michael. The building dates back to 1200, but its origins are Saxon. It takes its name from an Anglo-Saxon settlement on the banks of the Eden below, which was inundated when the river changed its course in 1350. A Viking 'hog back'

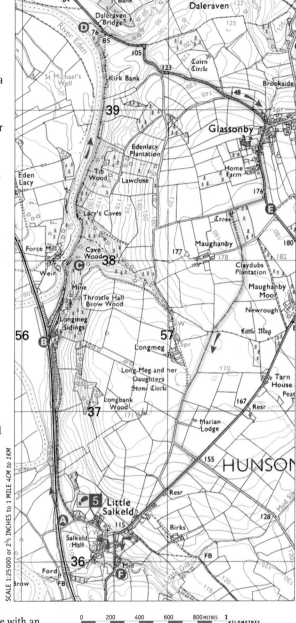

SCALE 1:25000 or 2½ INCHES to 1 MILE 4CM to 1KM

| 0 | 200 | 400 | 600 | 800 METRES | 1 |
| 0 | 200 | 400 | 600 YARDS | ½ |

KILOMETRES
MILES

tombstone, two halves of a 14th-century cross and two coffin lids, incised with early Christian emblems, were recovered from the river in 1930 and are now in the church porch. In the churchyard there is a good example of an Anglo-Saxon hammerhead cross.

Leave the churchyard by a gate onto the road to Maughanby Farm. Cross the road and follow the path over fields and through two gates, keeping a stone wall to your right. This leads to the site where Long Meg and her Daughters stand. Although far from dramatic, this is the second-largest neolithic circle in the country and is dated c. 1750 BC so is younger than Stonehenge. Long Meg is a 15ft (4.5m) megalith standing outside a slightly flattened circle of some sixty-nine large but low-standing stones. It is said that they are difficult to count and, should you get the number right, they will come to life or the devil will appear! When Colonel Lacy ordered them to be blown up with gunpowder and cut up to make milestones, the devil did appear – in the form of a terrifying thunderstorm – and the workmen fled in the belief that the druids were angry at the destruction of their temple. No one has tried to disturb them since. Whatever the purpose of this, one of many circles in Cumbria, at the winter solstice the sun, when visible, sets right on top of Meg's head like a halo. To witness this you must stand in the centre of the circle – if you can find it. It is most likely that the circle served as a calendar to mark the progression of the seasons, so important to a crop-growing community. It measures 342 by 305ft (104 by 93m), and the largest of the Daughters weighs 28 tons, with an average weight of 10 tons for the other stones. The site slopes, and it has been calculated that it would have needed sixty men to haul one stone $\frac{1}{2}$ mile (800m) to its position in the circle, so the whole site must have required 42,000 man-hours to complete. The population of this area at that time is estimated to have been about 2000 people.

Leave the circle along a continuation of the path from the church, which now becomes a metalled lane, and take the first turning left to the crossroad on the Glassonby–Little Salkeld road. From here the way leads to the right downhill for $\frac{1}{2}$ mile (800m) back into the village of Salkeld.

Keep going to the bridge over Little Gill, beside which is a restored, working water mill ⑤ that produces stone-ground flour from organically grown grain. About 4 tons of ten different flours are milled a week, some of which is sold in the adjacent shop. The working of the mill may be seen by appointment.

Winter solstice at Long Meg, Little Salkeld

Solway coast

Start	Port Carlisle
Distance	6 miles (9.7km)
Approximate time	4 hours
Parking	Port Carlisle
Refreshments	Pub at Port Carlisle, pub at Bowness-on-Solway (limited opening times)
Ordnance Survey maps	Landranger 85 (Carlisle & The Solway Firth), Pathfinder 544, NY 26/36 (Gretna & Eastriggs)

The Solway plain would appear to be flat and featureless, but there is much to see for those interested in the flora and fauna of the bog, saltings and estuarial mudflats, with the occasional bonus of beautiful Turneresque sunsets over the firth. On this walk, which is all on the level and therefore easy, there are the vanishing remains of a port and canal that once linked Carlisle to the sea, the last vestiges of the Roman wall, the village site of the most westerly and second largest fort on the wall, an expansive RSPB reserve for sea-birds and waders and, finally, a remote and little-known nature reserve of pools, bogs and gravel mounds. Walking on the marsh requires a lot of jumping over rivulets and water channels, so this is one walk for which wellies are virtually essential – and do not forget your binoculars.

Port Carlisle, originally called Fishers Cross, was developed as a port to handle cargoes for transhipment to Carlisle via a canal that was opened in 1823, only to close in 1853 when the deepwater channel in the firth shifted. It was then drained and a railway laid along its bed. It too has long since gone.

In the days of the canal, flyboats took passengers the 11 miles (17.5km) between port and city in two hours; the train was bit quicker. The station platform now provides a small car park by the bowling-green opposite the Hope and Anchor and extends to the front of Solway House, formerly the port's hotel. The main street is lined with pleasant Georgian houses, an

unexpected pleasure in so small a village. It was from Port Carlisle that President Woodrow Wilson's mother sailed for America.

Starting from the car park, walk back towards Carlisle, past a small chapel a little way out of the village and go through a kissing-gate **Ⓐ** on the left of the road, then bear left onto the foreshore of the Solway Firth. When the tide is out, a row of stunted piles can be seen marching across the mudflats to an elongated 'island', surrounded by a crumbling sandstone wall that lies 100 yds (91m) offshore. This was the deepwater dock, and the piles carried a tramway by which cargoes were transferred from ships to the canal barges lying alongside the harbour wall. The path along the waterfront passes the silted up sea lock, beyond which the first few yards of the old canal can be seen in water after high tides or heavy rain. Keep along the waterfront, past the Old Custom House to emerge on the road at the west end of the village. From here it is 1 mile (1.6km) across the marsh to Bowness-on-Solway, except at high tide, when the road must be used. The marsh is well endowed with salt-loving plants such as sea lavender, sea aster, thrift, scurvy, samphire and sea blight. Where the marsh ends, there is a slight promontory with a layby, frequently used by birdwatchers. The Scottish shore is $1\frac{1}{2}$ miles (2.4km) across the firth, which is sometimes a great expanse of water and at others a pattern of ever-changing channels in a sea of mud and sand. The last $\frac{1}{4}$ mile (400m) into Bowness-on-Solway must be made along the road as the foreshore from here on is sticky mud.

Bowness-on-Solway spreads over the site of a Roman fort, which around AD 250, had a garrison of 1000. Nothing remains of the fort, but its stones are incorporated in most of the old buildings in the village, especially the church **B**. A street map of the village with a plan of the fort superimposed on it can be studied on the wall of the King's Arms. St Michael's

Old quay at Port Carlisle, Solway Firth

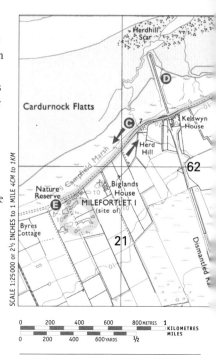

Church stands on the site of a Roman temple, and its most prized artefact is the 800-year-old font with interesting strap work, which was hidden in a grave during Cromwell's time. Soon after entering the village, a sign to The Banks takes you to a small landscaped part of the embankment above the water with a shelter for resting out of the wind and watching the birds. The village street climbs all of 40ft (12m) above sea-level before dropping down again past the school onto Campfield Marsh **C**, a 200-acre (80ha) RSPB reserve, on which pink-footed geese feed in winter, together with oyster-catchers, bar-tailed godwits, curlews, dunlins, knots, grey plovers and shelducks. In summer it is the home of breeding redshanks and lapwings.

There are miles of firm mud and sand to walk on, but a sharp eye must be kept for the returning tide which can fill unexpected channels between walker and dry land. A truncated viaduct **D**, which once carried a railway across the firth, runs out across the marsh. It is possible to walk out to the end of this feature and

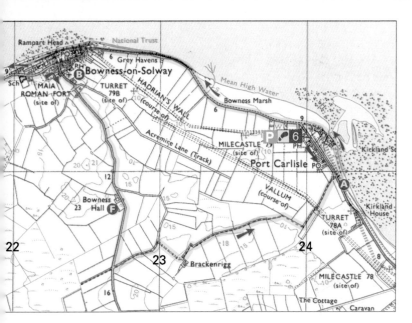

climb its stone sides to a viewpoint for skua in late April into May. But on no account walk out beyond or around the end of the viaduct where there are dangerous quicksands.

To get past the viaduct, go back onto the road that rises up and down over the line of the old railway. To the left one looks down on the old Bowness station, now a private house. About ½ mile (800m) on alongside the marsh, past first Biglands House farm and then a bungalow, there is a wooden gate **E**, giving access to a farm track that bisects the Bowness-on-Solway Nature Reserve, old gravel workings, managed by the Cumbria Wildlife Trust. Although only 16 acres (6.5ha), those with a bent for natural history might well wish to spend an hour or more wandering through its maze of paths, which wind through the heavy ground-cover and around the pools with duckboards crossing streams and boggy patches.

The return to Bowness-on-Solway is back along the road as far as the pub, where you turn right along the road past the church **B**. Continue on this road to Bowness Hall **F**, a typical Cumbrian farmhouse on the right, and ¼ mile

(400m) further on turn left at a footpath finger-post. This is an unmetalled road to Brackenrigg Farm, the final approach to which is along a concrete road. Go through the farm gate and immediately turn left into a green lane between high hedges. This leads by way of a couple of dog-legs to the little chapel at Port Carlisle, near the start of the walk. Along this green lane one gets a good view of the Solway Firth ahead and, over the hedgerows to the right, the somewhat bleak expanse of Glasson Moss, one of the most important raised bogs in the country. Just beyond the first dog-leg after Brackenrigg is the site of two Roman camps on the right of the lane, possibly used by the builders of Hadrian's Wall. The wall itself, of which there is now no sign, followed the line of the shore-side path going past the sea lock at the start of the walk.

At low water, binoculars can pick out the haaf-netters up to their chests in water fishing for sea trout and salmon with their hand-held 18ft- (5m) wide nets. Haaf is a Norse term, and this method of fishing has been practised here since Viking times. At the chapel, turn left to walk back into Port Carlisle.   ●

Hesket Newmarket and Caldbeck

Start	Hesket Newmarket
Distance	5 miles (8km)
Approximate time	2½ hours
Parking	Hesket Newmarket
Refreshments	Pubs and teashops at Hesket Newmarket and Caldbeck, restaurant at Caldbeck
Ordnance Survey maps	Landranger 90 (Penrith, Keswick & Ambleside), Pathfinder 576 NY 23/33 (Caldbeck)

The two small villages of Hesket Newmarket and Caldbeck are set 1 mile (1.6km) apart at the foot of the Caldbeck Fells, at the back of Blencathra and Skiddaw, Lakeland's most northerly mountains. This is John Peel country. He is buried in Caldbeck, and the surrounding fells where he walked and rode are criss-crossed with miners' tracks and dotted with disused shafts, for it was also lead- and copper-mining country. The two villages are connected by a walk along two becks, and outside Caldbeck yet another, the little Whelpo Beck, runs through The Howk, a limestone gorge with waterfalls and ruins of a great bobbin mill.

The start and finish of the walk is conveniently opposite the Old Crown **Ⓐ** in Hesket Newmarket. Follow a finger-posted footpath through a kissing-gate and across a field, alongside a tiny beck to a wooden footbridge and another kissing-gate. Go up a grass slope to yet another gate, beyond which turn sharp left and follow a narrow path above the beck, which soon joins the River Caldew. For some way the tree-clad bank is too high and too steep to climb down, but later it flattens out. In summer, fossils can be found in the dry river-bed. The path continues through a gate into a field, aiming for the corner of wire fencing ahead. From here, strike half-left towards two distinct trees isolated on high ground. Do *not* go straight ahead to the bridge that

crosses the Caldew as it is a dead-end. On reaching the two trees, bear slightly right past a wooden waymark-post and pass through a gate into a belt of trees above the river, which has curved round to meet you, and then follow the path down a flight of steps and onto a grassy ridge that curves right to a gate and stile on the edge of the wood.

The Cald Beck flows on one side of this ridge and the Caldew on the other – about 50 yds (46m) apart – but do not yet meet. Climb a stile into a wood and almost immediately cross a white wooden bridge **Ⓑ** on your left, spanning the Cald Beck. Instead of following the way along the riverbank, walk straight ahead up a slope from the bridge to join the forestry bridleway (the Cumbria Way), turning left

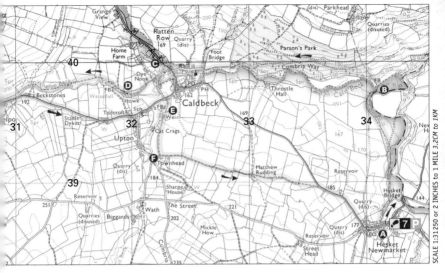

SCALE 1:31250 or 2 INCHES to 1 MILE 3.2CM to 1KM

into Caldbeck. Before the village, it becomes the service road for the sewage works, which leads to a bridge over the Caldew behind the church. On the far side of the bridge, a short, steep path on the right takes you down to the holy well that provides water for the font in St Kentigern's Church, part of which dates back to 1112. John Peel's marble gravestone with carved hunting symbols is in the churchyard. The wide street is lined with 18th-century houses, and on the village green there is a fine market cross with a bear-baiting ring. Visit also Priest's Mill with its mining museum and the lovely village pond **C**, where you will be greeted by at least a score of assorted quacking ducks.

Leave the village by the road alongside the pond and go through a red-painted wooden gate between two stone buildings; a small sign on one wall says 'To The Howk' **D**. The path leads through woods beside Whelpo Beck to the ruined bobbin mill in a gorge, but only the firm-footed should climb about the ruins. Particularly interesting is the cavity in which the waterwheel turned – it was the largest of its kind in England. A wooden leat from higher up the beck brought water across the top of the gorge to fall down the rockface to turn the wheel. The way continues

up a series of steps to a footbridge over a complex waterfall pouring into a cauldron below. The footpath accompanies the now quiescent beck to Whelpo Bridge. Cross this and turn left to walk back on a broad grass roadside verge towards Caldbeck.

After passing the primary school on the outskirts of the village, follow a Cumbria Way sign on the right, at the start of a row of cottages. It leads through a wicket gate on to a narrow lane and to a footbridge **E**. After crossing the bridge, go up a short, steep bank to a stile into a field. On a clear day, aim at High Pike, the obvious highest point on Caldbeck Fells ahead, otherwise follow the line of telephone-posts across the field and cross the wall by steps set into the stonework. Turn left past Townhead **F** along the lane to Matthew Rudding Farm. Go through the step stile in the stone wall at the north end of the farm buildings and, keeping close to the hedges, first on the left and then on the right, cross four fields and three stiles, before reaching steps in a stone wall beside the Caldbeck–Hesket Newmarket road. Here turn right on the road for the brief walk downhill into Hesket Newmarket.

Kentmere valley

Start	Kentmere
Distance	6½ miles (10.5km)
Approximate time	3½ hours
Parking	Small parking area by Kentmere church
Refreshments	None
Ordnance Survey maps	Landranger 90 (Penrith, Keswick & Ambleside), Outdoor Leisure 7 (The English Lakes – South Eastern area)

Although the narrow Kentmere valley is cradled by steep, rocky fells, this is a fairly level walk, following the western side of the valley from Kentmere church up to Kentmere Reservoir and returning along the eastern side. The outward track is well surfaced, but on the return leg you might encounter some boggy sections across low-lying riverside meadows. There is very much an off the beaten track feel about this walk in one of the less frequented parts of the Lake District.

The scattered hamlet of Kentmere comprises little more than a few farms, a hall that developed from a 14th-century peel tower and a simple church with a saddleback tower. The walk starts by the latter. Take the track beside the church, at a public footpath sign to Upper Kentmere and Kentmere Reservoir, and just before reaching the gateposts of a house, turn right through a gate and turn left along a tarmac track. The track soon becomes rough, heads steadily uphill, passing to the right of farms, and later levels off and continues above the valley.

Where the track bears right, keep ahead along a grassy track enclosed by walls, go through a gate and continue, later descending gently to go through another gate onto a tarmac track at the base of crags **Ⓐ**. Turn right and follow it through the valley, going through several gates and passing two farms – after the second farm it becomes a rough track. As you proceed through the valley the

countryside becomes emptier and more rugged. Go through more gates, later pass through disused slate quarries and, when you see a footbridge below **Ⓑ**, turn right to cross it. Turn left along a path that heads up to Kentmere Reservoir and turn right to follow a flat, grassy path across the dam. The view across the reservoir to the bare and lonely High Street range is particularly impressive.

On the other side of the dam, bear right to pass through a gap in the wall, ford a stream and turn right alongside a broken wall on the right to start the return leg. Follow the path below a quarry tip on the left and keep ahead through bracken to a ladder-stile. Climb it, continue across some badly drained ground to a newly renovated farmhouse, turn left through gateposts, turn right around the end of the building, turn left through a gate and turn right again to continue beside a wall on the right. Cross a footbridge, keep ahead, climb a ladder-stile and follow a path

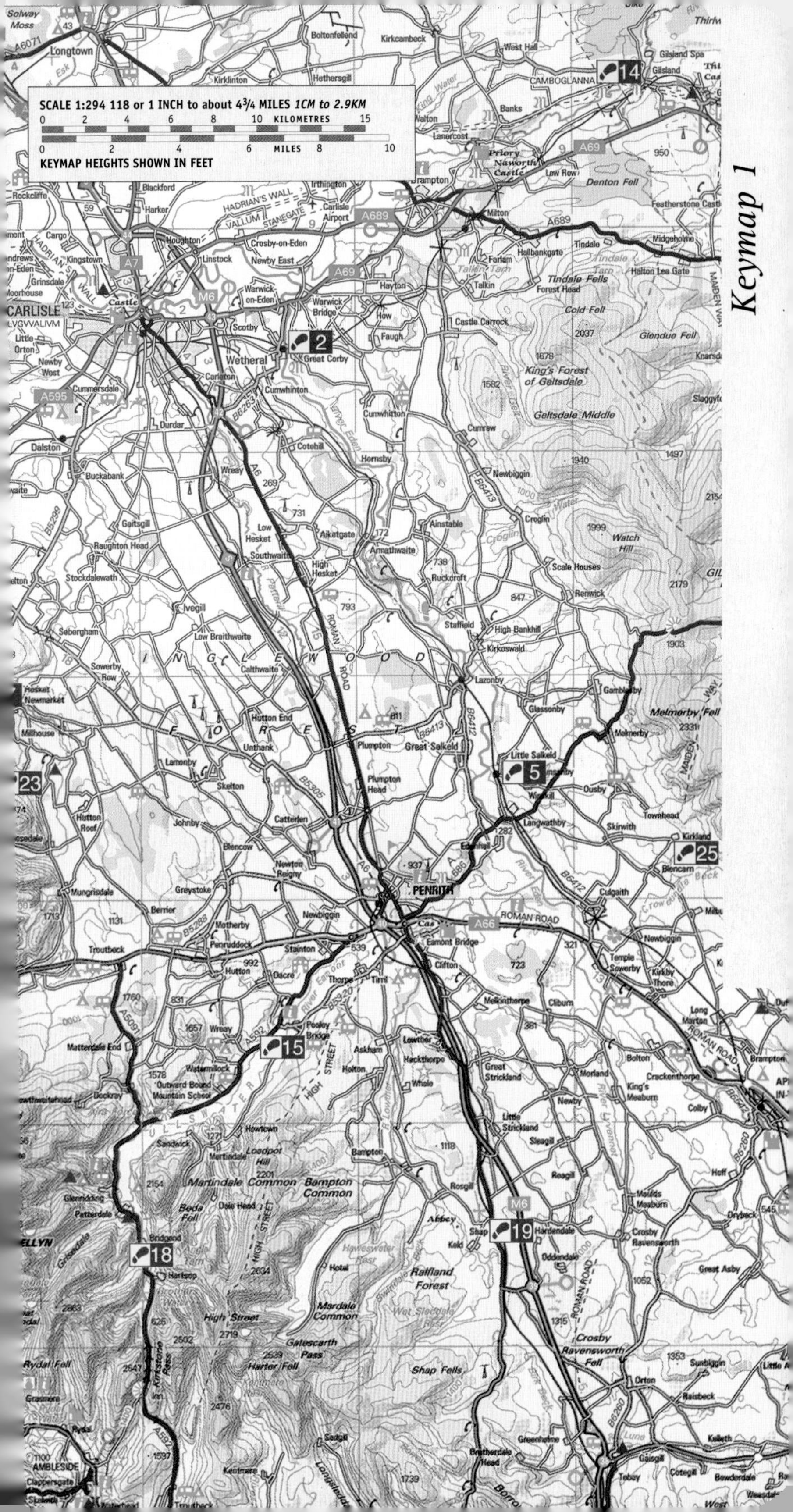

SCALE 1:294 118 or 1 INCH to about 4¾ MILES 1CM to 2.9KM
0 2 4 6 8 10 KILOMETRES 15
0 2 4 6 MILES 8 10
KEYMAP HEIGHTS SHOWN IN FEET
Solway Moss
Longtown
Boltonfellend
Kirkcambeck
West Hall
Gilsland Spa
Gilsland
CAMBOGLANNA
14
Kirklinton
Hethersgill
Banks
Walton
Lanercost
Priory
Naworth Castle
Low Row
Denton Fell
Brampton
Rockcliffe
Blackford
Irthington
Harker
HADRIAN'S WALL
VALLUM
STANEGATE
Carlisle Airport
A689
Milton
Featherstone Castle
Houghton
Crosby-on-Eden
Kingstown
Linstock
Newby East
Farlam
Hallbankgate
Tindale
Midgeholme
Tindale Tarn
Halton Lea Gate
Talkin Tarn
Talkin
Tindale Fells
Forest Head
Grinsdale
Moorhouse
Warwick-on-Eden
Hayton
A69
CARLISLE
LVGVVALIVM
Castle
Warwick Bridge
How
Castle Carrock
Cold Fell
2037
Glendue Fell
Scotby
Faugh
Little Orton
2
Great Corby
Newby West
Wetheral
1678
King's Forest of Geltsdale
River Gelt
Carleton
Cumwhinton
1582
Cummersdale
A595
Cumwhitton
Geltsdale Middle
Durdar
Currew
Dalston
Cotehill
Hornsby
1940
1497
Buckabank
Wreay
269
Newbiggin
B6413
731
Low Hesket
Aiketgate
172
Ainstable
Croglin
Croglin Water
1999
Watch Hill
Gaitsgill
Raughton Head
Southwaite
Armathwaite
High Hesket
738
Scale Houses
Stockdalewath
Ruckcroft
2179
River Petteril
847
Renwick
793
Ivegill
ROMAN ROAD
Staffield
High Bankhill
Sebergham
Low Braithwaite
Kirkoswald
1903
INGLEWOOD FOREST
Sowerby Row
Calthwaite
Lazonby
Gamblesby
Hesket Newmarket
B6412
Melmerby Fell
Hutton End
811
Glassonby
Millhouse
Unthank
Plumpton
Great Salkeld
Melmerby
2331
Lamonby
Little Salkeld
MAIDEN WAY
5
Skelton
Plumpton Head
Winskill
Ousby
23
B5305
Langwathby
Hutton Roof
Catterlen
282
Townhead
Skirwith
Johnby
Blencow
Edenhall
Kirkland
25
Newton Reigny
937
Blencarn
A6
PENRITH
B6412
Culgaith
Crowdundle Beck
Mungrisdale
Greystoke
River Eden
1713
1131
Berrier
Newbiggin
ROMAN ROAD
Castle
A66
Newbiggin
Motherby
B5288
Penruddock
Eamont Bridge
Troutbeck
Stainton
539
321
723
Temple Sowerby
992
Hutton
Dacre
Clifton
Kirkby Thore
Thorpe
Tirril
River Eamont
B5320
1760
831
Melkinthorpe
Cliburn
A5091
1657
Wreay
Pooley Bridge
361
Long Marton
ROMAN ROAD
Matterdale End
A592
15
Askham
Lowther
Great Strickland
Bolton
Brampton
1578
Watermillock
Helton
Hackthorpe
Outward Bound Mountain School
Whale
Morland
Crackenthorpe
Dockray
Newby
King's Meaburn
ULLSWATER
HIGH STREET
Colby
Howtown
River Lowther
Little Strickland
River Lyvennet
B6260
Sandwick
1271
Loadpot Hill
1118
Martindale
2201
Sleagill
Bampton
Bampton Common
Martindale Common
2154
Reagill
Hoff
Glenridding
Rosgill
Patterdale
Beda Fell
Dale Head
M6
Maulds Meaburn
Drybeck
545
Abbey
Shap
19
Hardendale
Crosby Ravensworth
HELLYN
Bridgend
18
Keld
Oddendale
Haweswater Resr
Hartsop
2634
Hotel
Ralfland Forest
ROMAN ROAD
1052
Great Asby
Swindale
2863
Mardale Common
Wet Sleddale Resr
625
High Street
2502
2719
1315
Gatescarth Pass
2539
Crosby Ravensworth Fell
Rydal Fell
2547
Kirkstone Pass
Harter Fell
Shap Fells
1353
Sunbiggin
Little Asby
Grasmere
Kentmere Resr
Orton
2476
Raisbeck
Rydal
Greenholme
Kelleth
1100
AMBLESIDE
1597
Sadgill
Borrowdale
Bretherdale Head
Gaisgill
Clappersgate
Kentmere
1739
Tebay
Cotegill
Bowderdale
Longsleddale
Borrow Beck
River Lune
Wester

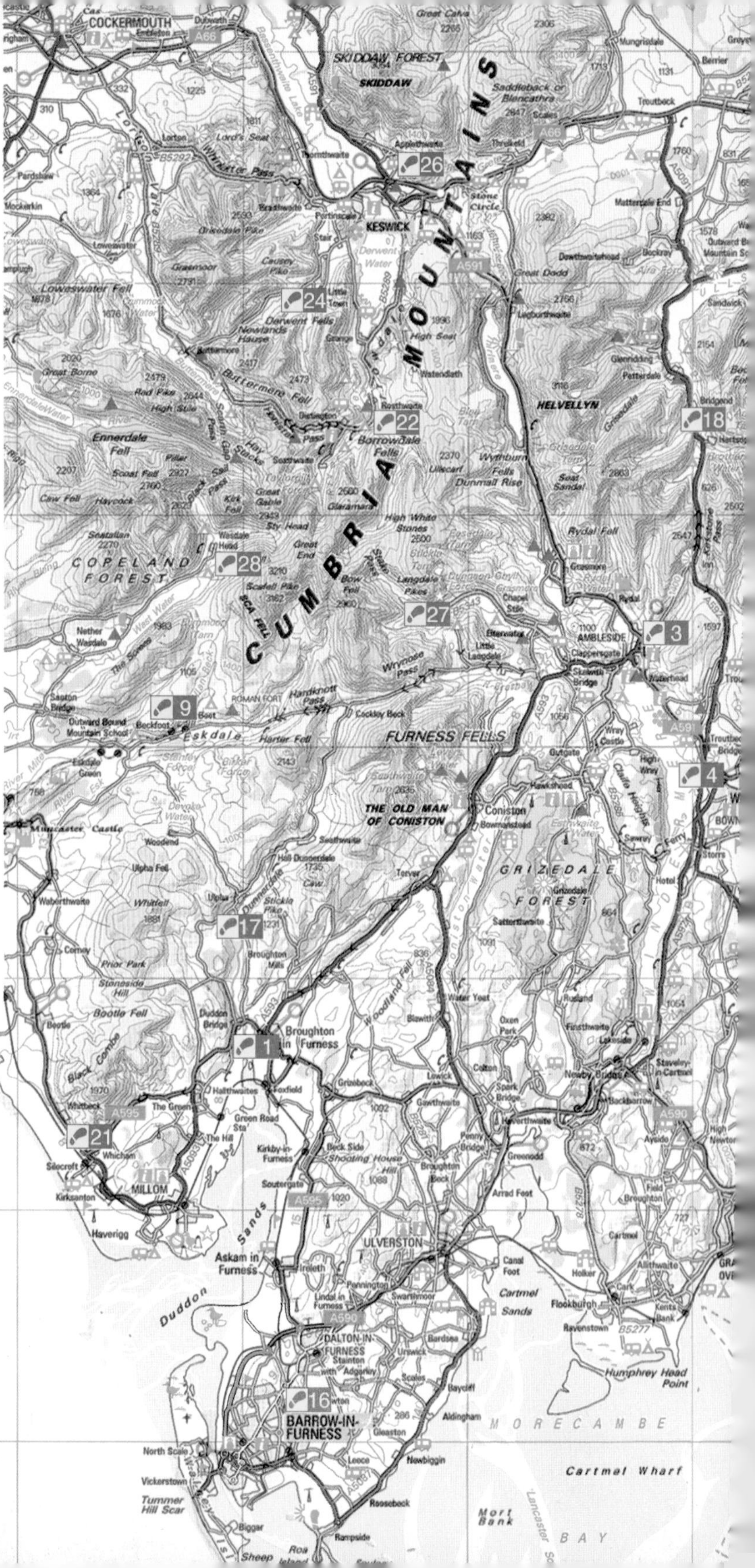

COCKERMOUTH

SKIDDAW, FOREST
SKIDDAW

Saddleback or
Blencathra

[26]

KESWICK

CUMBRIA MOUNTAINS

[24]

HELVELLYN

[18]

[22]
Borrowdale
Fells

COPELAND
FOREST

[28]

[27]

[3]
AMBLESIDE

[9]
Eskdale

FURNESS FELLS

[4]

THE OLD MAN
OF CONISTON

Coniston

GRIZEDALE
FOREST

[17]

Broughton
in Furness

[1]

[21]

MILLOM

ULVERSTON

Duddon
Sands

DALTON-IN-
FURNESS

[16]

BARROW-IN-
FURNESS

MORECAMBE

Cartmel Wharf

Mort
Bank

BAY

Keymap 2

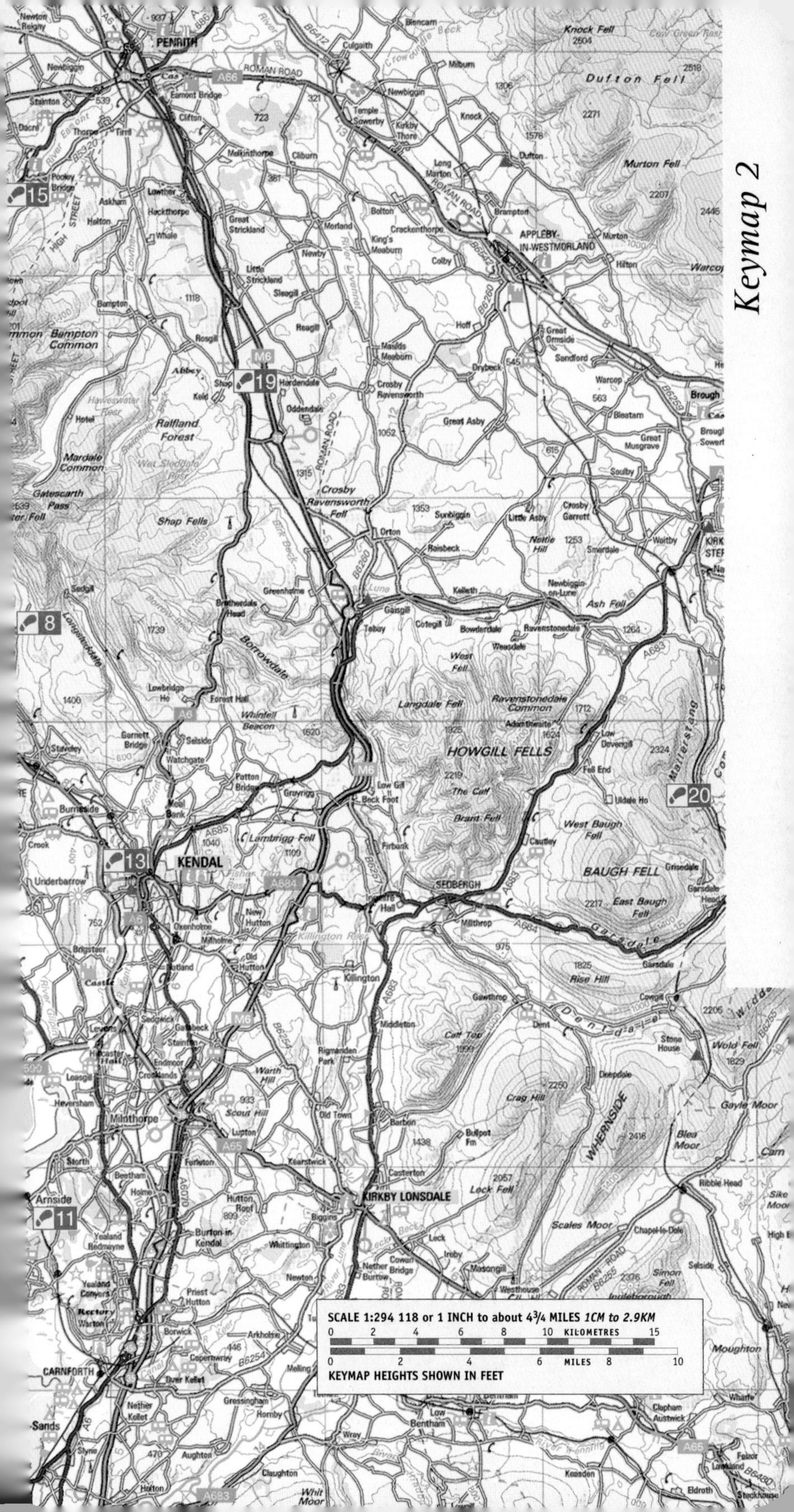

PENRITH
APPLEBY-IN-WESTMORLAND
KENDAL
SEDBERGH
KIRKBY LONSDALE
CARNFORTH
HOWGILL FELLS
BAUGH FELL
WHERNSIDE
Dufton Fell
Murton Fell
Knock Fell
Shap Fells
Crosby Ravensworth Fell
Ralfland Forest
Mardale Common
Bampton Common
Langdale Fell
Ravenstonedale Common
Rise Hill
Dentdale
Lambrigg Fell
Scout Hill
Lock Fell
Scales Moor
Gayle Moor
Blea Moor
Wold Fell
Crag Hill
Calf Top
Borrowdale
Whinfell Beacon
Mallerstang
Garsdale
Orton
Tebay
Shap
Milnthorpe
Arnside
Burton-in-Kendal
Bentham
Ingleborough
SCALE 1:294 118 or 1 INCH to about 4¾ MILES 1CM to 2.9KM
0 2 4 6 8 10 KILOMETRES 15
0 2 4 6 MILES 8 10
KEYMAP HEIGHTS SHOWN IN FEET

transferred from ships to the canal barges lying alongside the harbour wall. The path along the waterfront passes the silted up sea lock, beyond which the first few yards of the old canal can be seen in water after high tides or heavy rain. Keep along the waterfront, past the Old Custom House to emerge on the road at the west end of the village. From here it is 1 mile (1.6km) across the marsh to Bowness-on-Solway, except at high tide, when the road must be used. The marsh is well endowed with salt-loving plants such as sea lavender, sea aster, thrift, scurvy, samphire and sea blight. Where the marsh ends, there is a slight promontory with a layby, frequently used by birdwatchers. The Scottish shore is 1½ miles (2.4km) across the firth, which is sometimes a great expanse of water and at others a pattern of ever-changing channels in a sea of mud and sand. The last ¼ mile (400m) into Bowness-on-Solway must be made along the road as the foreshore from here on is sticky mud.

Bowness-on-Solway spreads over the site of a Roman fort, which around AD 250, had a garrison of 1000. Nothing remains of the fort, but its stones are incorporated in most of the old buildings in the village, especially the church Ⓑ. A street map of the village with a plan of the fort superimposed on it can be studied on the wall of the King's Arms. St Michael's

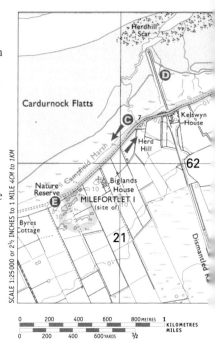

SCALE 1:25 000 or 2½ INCHES to 1 MILE 4CM to 1KM

Church stands on the site of a Roman temple, and its most prized artefact is the 800-year-old font with interesting strap work, which was hidden in a grave during Cromwell's time. Soon after entering the village, a sign to The Banks takes you to a small landscaped part of the embankment above the water with a shelter for resting out of the wind and watching the birds. The village street climbs all of 40ft (12m) above sea-level before dropping down again past the school onto Campfield Marsh Ⓒ, a 200-acre (80ha) RSPB reserve, on which pink-footed geese feed in winter, together with oyster-catchers, bar-tailed godwits, curlews, dunlins, knots, grey plovers and shelducks. In summer it is the home of breeding redshanks and lapwings.

There are miles of firm mud and sand to walk on, but a sharp eye must be kept for the returning tide which can fill unexpected channels between walker and dry land. A truncated viaduct Ⓓ, which once carried a railway across the firth, runs out across the marsh. It is possible to walk out to the end of this feature and

Old quay at Port Carlisle, Solway Firth

across a meadow. Pass between gateposts, continue across the next meadow to meet the River Kent again and then continue beside it along a pleasant tree-lined track.

Go through a gate, keep ahead along a track across a meadow, veering slightly left away from the river, go through another gate and continue by a wall on the left. After the next gate, keep by a wall on the right, and later the track becomes enclosed between walls. Pass to the left of a farm and, at a junction of tracks by the farm buildings, go through a metal gate and walk along the right-hand, lower track to a wooden gate. Go through this and continue along a path just above the valley bottom that heads gently downhill, later keeping beside a low, partly broken wall and line of trees on the right, to a gate. Go through and keep ahead, by a wall on the right, to join and continue along a track called Low Lane. After crossing a footbridge, at a public bridleway sign to Kentmere, the track becomes narrower and enclosed. Keep along it and, about 100 yds (91m) after passing through a second gate at the top of a slight rise, look out for where there are stone stiles on both sides 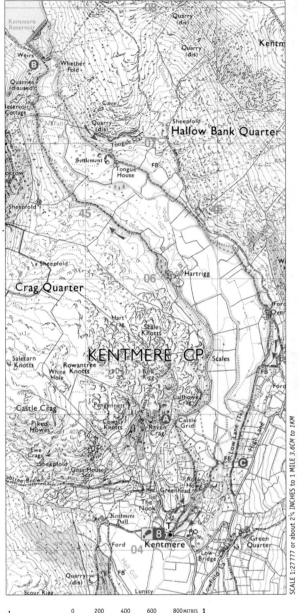.

Climb the stile on the right and follow a path downhill to meet and keep by a wall on the right. Turn right to cross a footbridge over the river, keep ahead and climb a stone stile onto a walled track.

SCALE 1:27777 or about 2¼ INCHES to 1 MILE 3.6CM to 1KM

0	200	400	600	800 METRES	1	
					KILOMETRES	MILES
0	200	400	600 YARDS	½		

Turn left along it to a farm, go through a gate to the left of farm buildings and, at a fork a few yards ahead, continue along the left-hand, lower track, which leads directly back to Kentmere church. On joining a tarmac track, bear left along it to a T-junction and turn right beside the church to return to the start.

Boot

Start	Dalegarth Station, Boot
Distance	4¼ miles (6.8km)
Approximate time	2¼ hours
Parking	Station car park at Dalegarth, near Boot
Refreshments	Café at Dalegarth Station, pub and café at Boot, Woolpack Inn to east of point D
Ordnance Survey maps	Landranger 89 (West Cumbria), Outdoor Leisure 6 (The English Lakes – South Western area)

The valley of the River Esk is among the loveliest and possibly least disturbed in the Lake District. Apart from La'al Ratty, the narrow-gauge railway whose steam trains carry visitors up and down the first 7 miles (11.3km), there has been no tourist development so its pleasures are all natural ones, not least its riverside and fellside walks. This walk starts with a gentle stroll uphill past a series of waterfalls before crossing open moorland, from where there are grand panoramas of some of the finest Lakeland mountains, including the Sca Fell group and Great Gable. After reaching a little tarn set among hills, the way descends steeply, with expansive views of stone farmhouses in a pattern of neatly walled fields along the Esk valley, and ends with a level walk beside the river. There is no rough terrain, and the height reached should be safe in all weather, but walking-shoes or boots are recommended, as is protective clothing against the wind chill above the valley.

From Dalegarth Station **Ⓐ** turn left along the road to Brook House and left again up the lane to Boot and Eskdale Mill. The first stop on the walk could be at Eskdale Mill just up the lane beside the bridge over Whillan Beck. It has been working since 1578 and still does when it has visitors, who – strangely for so interesting a place – are rather few. Almost as fascinating as its complex internal workings is the system that diverts water from higher up the beck, which is controlled by sluices and fed to a 12ft (3.7m) overshot wheel by a wooden leat. A path through the woods

follows the course of this water system.

Through a gate just beyond the mill, turn left onto the fell to see what was once the terminus of the Ravenglass and Eskdale Railway, which was built originally to service Nab Gill iron ore mines near the top of the fell above Boot. Down the fellside there is what looks like a great smudge of pink paint. This is spillage of haematite, or iron ore, along the line of the self-acting inclined railway that used to bring the ore down to the then 3ft- (1m) gauge railway. A cable ran round a wheel at the top of the incline,

SCALE 1:25000 or 2½ INCHES to 1 MILE 4CM to 1KM

0	200	400	600	800 METRES	1
					KILOMETRES
					MILES
0	200	400	600 YARDS	½	

and loaded wagons running down pulled a string of empty ones up to the top to be loaded. At the foot of the now much decayed and overgrown incline the layout of Boot Station with its passenger platform and ore-loading bays can still be made out. The shell of a stone building was the mine manager's office. A low circular stone-walled enclosure is the remains of the store for gunpowder, which was used until 1874, when it was replaced by Alfred Nobel's new dynamite. The mines closed down in 1882.

From this site of industrial archaeology go back over the bridge, turn left up a gated lane beside two holiday cottages and walk up beside Whillan Beck. For some way the beck is a succession of falls **B** where, except when in full spate in winter, it is possible to walk about on great slabs of rock with the water rushing and tumbling around you. The point at which the falls can be easily reached is about 200 yds (183m) from the start of the lane opposite a gate on the right. The lane continues as a good farm road to Gill Bank, but halfway there a public footpath sign to Eel Tarn directs you through a gate and then another sign leads uphill to the left on a rough, stony path. This path continues with a slight curve all the way round the crags of Little Barrow, Great Barrow and Little Pie. On the way, one is treated to a clear view of the southern side of Sca Fell with Great Gable peeping over its shoulder on the left. Scafell Pike is hidden behind the fell. Near a high point on the path it is crossed by a small stream, and a course should be taken to the right **C** about 50 yds (45m) beyond the stream and parallel to it. This is a fairly obvious grass way over a shallow shoulder, beyond which is Eel Tarn. This is a pretty piece of water decorated with water-lilies and lying in a peaty basin surrounded by bobbing cotton grass and boulders, the latter providing seats for a rest or picnic.

At the far end of the tarn a clearly marked peat and grass path starts to wind gently between rock outcrops down the hillside to the road on the valley bottom. For most of the way there are oblique views up and down the middle of Eskdale with the steep high rock faces of Birker, Harter and Ulpha fells forming the far horizon. Shoulder-high bracken softens the immediate scene and gives a feeling of protection against the ever-present, looming crags above. Eventually the path comes out onto the road beside the Woolpack Inn. Here, turn right and almost immediately left **D** along the lane to Penny Hill Farm but, instead of crossing the stone Doctor Bridge to the farm, keep on the path alongside the Esk all the way to St Catherine's Church on the riverbank. It is a relatively level and pleasant walk, always within sight or sound of the pebble-strewn river. Gill Force is in a little ravine with deep pools that attract hardy divers into the cold mountain water. St Catherine's Church is well over 600 years old but was largely rebuilt in 1881 at the enormous cost of £750, equivalent to the incumbent's stipend for ten years. Until 1901 the churchyard was the burial ground for both Eskdale and Wasdale. The rough track that runs from Wasdale Head up to Burnmoor Tarn and then down beside the iron ore mines, now a popular fell walk, was until early in this century maintained as a corpse road. Follow the walled lane that runs up from the church past Eskview Farm to the crossroads at Brook House and turn left along the road to return to the start. ●

Track from Boot to Eel Tarn, Eskdale

St Bees Head

Start	St Bees seafront car park
Distance	6½ miles (10.5km)
Approximate time	4 hours
Parking	Seafront car park
Refreshments	Hotel, pubs and cafés at St Bees, pub at Sandwith
Ordnance Survey maps	Landranger 89 (West Cumbria), Pathfinder 593, NX 90/91 (Whitehaven & St Bees)

To walkers, St Bees is best known as the starting point of the 190-mile (306km) Coast to Coast Walk, which finishes at Robin Hood's Bay, and for the 400ft (122m) cliffs of St Bees Head, where this walk starts. The cliff walk is also along the edge of an RSPB nature reserve, and there are several viewing-points along the way where seabirds can be watched on the cliff ledges, though those with a fear of vertigo might like to choose a different walk. When the air is clear, the Galloway Hills of Scotland, the Isle of Man and sometimes the Mountains of Mourne in Northern Ireland are visible.

St Bees is a small seaside resort with a long shingle beach. In the old part of the town is the medieval Church of Sts Mary and Bega, once part of a priory. Opposite is St Bees Grammar School, founded 1587.

At the north end of St Bees promenade there is a lifeboat house. Beyond it a metal bridge over Rottington Beck takes you onto the pebble beach, which you cross to a stile at the start of the path to the cliff top. This is a relentless climb of 400ft (122m) in less than a ½ mile (800m), but steps have been cut into the steepest sections. If the sun is shining and the sky blue, the views out to sea are superb. At the summit at South Head Ⓐ and for some way along there is rarely more than a foot or

two between you and the cliff face, but fear of vertigo is allayed by the thick cushion of bracken hiding the actual edge. Most of the time you can see the lighthouse on North Head, but it is lost to view as the path starts descending towards the beach at Fleswick, before

Path down to Fleswick Cove, St Bees Head

turning sharply inland down a stepped path to the bottom of the gully and an isolated pebble beach under the cliffs. In the gully there are two stiles to cross, before making the ascent up the other side.

There is a choice of two paths to the top of the cliff again. One, about a foot wide, traverses the grass-covered side of the gully and is quite unprotected. The lower one, which is preferable, takes a gentler gradient, then goes up some steps, all the while alongside a fence. Having gained the cliff top, there is a white-painted bench awaiting those who would rest a while and take in the view of the cliffs left behind, with the blue sea one way and the bright green of the field system the other. The path continues slightly uphill, with the ground on the right now much flatter, and there is no longer a sense of being hemmed in. Soon after passing the bright white wall around the lighthouse, the cliffs bend round to the north-east, and Saltom Bay opens up ahead with the entrance to Whitehaven harbour plain to see. The path wanders in and out round several indentations and in places it again runs near the cliff edge.

Soon after passing two waymark-posts and crossing a stile, you come to a path off to the right **B**, reached over a second stile. This follows the left-hand edge of a field to join an overgrown farm track, which in turn meets a road by a radio mast, which is just beyond a small reservoir **C**. Turn left down the road beside the reservoir and go all the way into the village of Sandwith. Leave the village on the road north and at the Lanehead junction follow the road signposted to Demesne, waymarked in green. This is a truly rural little lane between high hedgerows zigzagging down to Demesne Farm. Turn right through the farm following the Coast to Coast Walk signpost **D**, cross the Whitehaven road and go down the lane to Bell House. It is

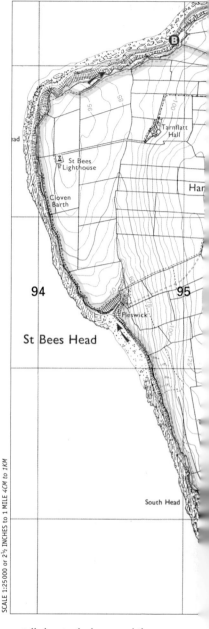

SCALE 1:25000 or 2½ INCHES to 1 MILE 4CM to 1KM

metalled up to the house and then becomes a farm track, contouring the hillside before falling away towards the corner **E** of Abbey Wood. To the right, the rising ground shuts out all views, but on the left one looks up and down the broad valley along which the railway track runs parallel and equidistant with the path all the way into St Bees. In places the path is overgrown and has quite

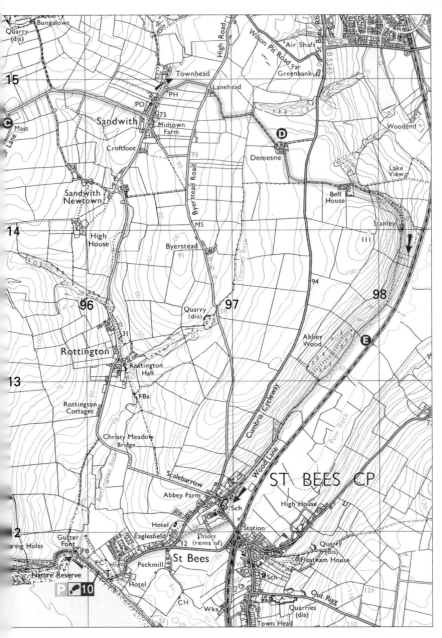

disappeared. Head for the edge of the wood, where two stiles have to be climbed, one on either side of a little gully with a watercourse running down it.

Alongside the wood, the route is through long grass, continuing like this until a gate leads into Wood Lane, where there is a stile into the car park of St Bees School. Walk on between the school buildings and come out on the road into the town. Turn left towards the railway station, then leave the road at the public footpath sign on the right, walk across a field and go through a gate onto the upper road. Turn left and keep on the road, passing the big white hotel on the front, and bear right to the car park. ●

Arnside Knott and Tower

Start	Arnside
Distance	6 miles (9.7km)
Approximate time	3 hours
Parking	Promenade at Arnside
Refreshments	Pubs and cafés at Arnside
Ordnance Survey maps	Landranger 97 maps (Kendal & Morecambe), Pathfinder 636, SD 37/47 (Grange-over-Sands)

The tremendous scenic variety on this relatively short walk includes meadowland, woodland, open hillside, low cliffs, coastal marshes and the estuary of the River Kent. There are some beautiful stretches of woodland fringing Morecambe Bay and the Kent estuary and on the slopes of Arnside Knott, and the undemanding climb to the 522ft (159m) summit of the latter, now owned by the National Trust, provides a glorious panoramic view over Morecambe Bay and the Lakeland mountains.

The coming of the Furness Railway in the middle of the 19th century killed off Arnside's role as a small port but gave it a new lease of life as a quiet holiday resort. Its most prominent feature, apart from the Knott on the south side of the town, is the embankment and viaduct across the Kent estuary, the latter constructed in 1857 and resting on fifty piers.

The walk starts at the far end of the promenade. Take the shore path above the Kent estuary, at a public footpath sign New Barns Bay, and just before reaching a coastguard station bear left **Ⓐ** up an enclosed tarmac path, signposted Knott Road and Silverdale, to a road. Turn right along it and at a fork take the left-hand lane that becomes narrower as it ascends Arnside Knott, a steady climb. About 50 yds (45m) after squeezing through a gap beside a gate and cattle-grid, turn left, by a view indicator board, and follow a stony path steeply uphill to the summit **Ⓑ**, marked by a stone shelter and series

of indicator boards. The view over the Kent estuary, Lakeland fells, Furness peninsula and Morecambe Bay surpasses that from considerably higher peaks.

Continue past the summit along a path, which after a few yards enters trees, and follow it through woodland. By a stile in a wall the path turns right and keeps alongside the wall on the left, descending through most attractive woodland to a stile. Climb it onto a road, turn right – Arnside Tower can be seen ahead – and after ¼ mile (400m) turn left onto a tarmac farm track, at a footpath sign to Silverdale **Ⓒ**. At the farm bear right, passing to the right of the farm buildings, go through a metal gate and at a public footpath sign bear left, in the Silverdale and Tower direction, up to the tower. Arnside Tower was one of a chain of peel towers built around Morecambe Bay in the 14th century to protect the area from Scottish coastal raids; part of it blew down in a great gale in 1602.

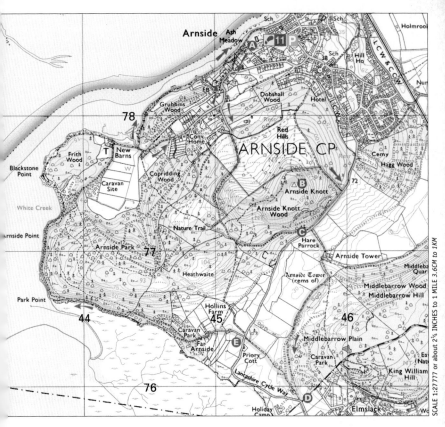

Do not climb the ladder-stile in front but turn right to climb a stone stile to the left of a metal gate and walk along a hedge-lined track, by woodland on the left. Go through a metal gate, continue along the track and, on reaching a tarmac drive, bear left, at a yellow waymark, along the left-hand of two parallel drives that pass through a caravan site. At a T-junction of drives, turn right towards shop and café and at a public footpath sign turn right again, in the Far Arnside direction **D**. On entering trees, bear left off the drive, at a yellow waymark, along a path through the trees, later continuing across grass to go through a metal gate. Keep ahead, go through a kissing-gate, continue along the left-hand edge of a field, by a wall on the left, and go through another kissing-gate onto a lane **E**.

Cross over, walk along the lane opposite, passing attractive cottages, and continue through Far Arnside Caravan Park, following footpath signs to White Creek. Where the tarmac drive ends, keep ahead along a path through woodland and, at a fork by a public footpath sign, take the left-hand path that descends to a gate. Go through and continue along an attractive stretch through coastal woodlands, following a line of low cliffs above Morecambe Bay. Later the path turns right to continue by the Kent estuary.

Where the path forks at a footpath sign, keep ahead along the main path through woodland, shortly curving left through another caravan site and following signs to Arnside. Bear left to join a tarmac track, follow it to a T-junction and turn right along the edge of a creek. On the other side is a choice: either continue along the track (advisable if the tide is in) or bear left to follow the shore back to Arnside. ●

Cockermouth and the Derwent valley

Start	Cockermouth
Distance	7½ miles (12.1km)
Approximate time	3 hours
Parking	Riverside Car Park at Cockermouth
Refreshments	Hotels, restaurants, pubs and cafés at Cockermouth
Ordnance Survey maps	Landranger 89 (West Cumbria), Outside Leisure 4 (The English Lakes – North Western area)

The River Cocker, from which Cockermouth takes its name, is now largely canalised and hidden behind houses. It flows unnoticed into the broad and elegant Derwent, which circles the north of the town. This walk, which is part of the Allerdale Ramble, takes a scenic route to Isel Bridge and back, offering views of the verdant Derwent valley. The tree-hung river runs between multi-hued green slopes of pastures, dotted with sheep and divided by the soft lines of bushy hedges and trees.

The town of Cockermouth has much of interest, not least the house where Wordsworth was brought up until the age of thirteen with his sister Dorothy and three brothers. He wrote of the Derwent: 'It is the fairest of all rivers', which may be a slight exaggeration, but it is renowned for its trout. Above the confluence of the Derwent and Cocker stands the medieval castle, built to protect the local area from marauding Scots. Fletcher Christian of the *Bounty* mutiny was born locally and went to the same local school as Wordsworth. Small yards and alleyways with interesting shops lead off the main street that forms an attractive boulevard. Both town and river are overlooked from the south by the heights of Fellbarrow, Whin Fell and Kirk Fell.

Start the walk from the Riverside Car Park on the north bank of the Cocker, walking past the Derwent Mill sign to a

T-junction with a path alongside a wall. Turn right and then left up a green lane and go over a stile into a meadow. Follow the line of electricity poles uphill to a gate with stone steps to one side. Once over these, keep alongside a fence, aiming at a stand of trees higher up. Climb over two more sets of steps in short lengths of high stone walls at the end of thick hedges to reach a meadow, sloping down to a farm road **Ⓐ**. Cross the road, go up the opposite meadow, over one more stile, then keep over to the right towards the final stile onto the A595 to Carlisle. Turn right, being careful of the fast-moving traffic.

Having gained height on that first part of the walk, you can look down on Cockermouth and over to the high hills beyond. After passing a house on the left, you soon come to a layby **Ⓑ** on the right. Climb over a stile here and walk left, then

St Michael's Church in Isel, near Cockermouth

right, around the perimeter of an arable field. Soon a stile on your left leads into a large meadow. Cross it towards the near corner of a line of trees and keep beside the wood, go through a gap in a hedge to a second field and, at the far end of the wood, cross another stile. Bear slightly left to walk around the base of Park Hill to meet a tractor track coming up from Redmain Hall Farm. After passing through a gate into the farmyard, go up a short farm drive to a road. Turn right through the village and, and a few yards beyond the last house there is a signpost **C** to Isel, on the right pointing into the bushes. There is a tiny bit of path down to a hawthorn bush, which, when pushed aside, reveals an ancient gap stile.

This is the start of another short cross-country path. There is a trodden way alongside the wall running downhill from the stile, but ignore this and follow the line of the right-of-way on the map. Walk diagonally uphill to the left across a meadow, down a sharp drop to a gate in another wall, across a second meadow, a dried-up watercourse and down into Gill Wood. Look for the wooden stile into the wood and then follow a wandering path through the trees and over a couple of footbridges to the road. Turn right here and walk down to Isel. At the start of the

village just over a stone bridge is Isel Grange, a country-house painted in Hapsburg yellow and looking rather grand and unusual in these parts. Further on you get glimpses through the trees of Isel Hall, tucked away behind a stone wall, but neither grounds nor house is open to the public. This embattled manor-house with peel tower, c. 1425, has been the home of the Lawson family for over 400 years. One member, Sir Wilfrid, was a hunting colleague of John Peel.

From Isel the road runs downhill to Isel Bridge over the Derwent, from where there is a grand view of the river, which leads the eye to the full shape of Skiddaw to the east. Before crossing the bridge, make a short detour down a lane to St Michael's Church **D**, said to be half as old as Christendom, sitting in its ancient graveyard surrounded by a stone wall. The oldest part of the church, built about 1130, is best recognised by the small slit windows on the north side. The font is estimated to date from about 1275, and the bells under the west window were possibly caste by an itinerant founder around 1375. The fifteen windows, a large number for a small church, progress in size as the church was modified and restored over the centuries to the largest, the west window, installed in 1878. There was certainly an even earlier church, perhaps a mere cross and then a wattle

| 0 | 200 | 400 | 600 | 800 METRES | 1 |
| 0 | 200 | 400 | 600 YARDS | ½ | KILOMETRES MILES |

shelter. The area was then thickly forested with oaks, and the River Derwent would have been an important means of transport and communication. Beyond the bridge, the road rises up from the river to the junction with the road back to Cockermouth. Turn right and walk on until you come to a gate on the left, leading to a bridleway veering away from the road. This is a substantial forestry-

type road, which climbs gently, offering more fine views over the Derwent valley. There are no mountains, no great hills and certainly no spreads of water, but the Lake District scenery returns before the walk ends.

Going along the edge of Hill's Wood, it is easy to forget the map and absent-mindedly continue on the forestry road as it takes a bend to the left to double back on itself. Keep to the bridleway **E**, which continues in a straight line but as a narrower path, no longer like a road. It is

SCALE 1:25000 or 2½ INCHES to 1 MILE 4CM to 1KM

rough and stony, but close inspection shows that the stones were originally laid to form a slight camber at the time when it was used by carts if not carriages. Emerging from the shade of the woodland, the way rises for a while longer, goes over a stile and round the corner of a stone wall near the summit of Watch Hill, and there below lies the whole of Cockermouth. From here on, it is downhill all the way, partly on a grass path and later a more eroded farm track, over several stiles to the road into the town.

Arriving at the fork in the road into the town, it is more interesting to take the left-hand one that leads down to St Helen's Street, then into Market Place and, further on, Main Street, after crossing a bridge over the Cocker. Walk along Main Street, past the statue of the Earl of Mayo in the middle of the road and the Wordsworth Centre in a former church on the left, to Bridge Street, a vehicular cul-de-sac. The Riverside Car Park is reached over a pedestrian suspension bridge. ●

Kendal, Scout Scar and Cunswick Fell

Start	Kendal
Distance	7 miles (11.3km)
Approximate time	3½ hours
Parking	Kendal
Refreshments	Pubs and cafés at Kendal
Ordnance Survey maps	Landranger 97 (Kendal & Morecambe), Outdoor Leisure 7 (The English Lakes – South Eastern area)

This is a walk in the limestone country that lies on the south-eastern fringes of the Lake District. From Kendal the route heads up out of the town and continues by way of field and moorland paths to the edge of the escarpment of Scout Scar, a superb viewpoint looking westwards towards the central Lakeland mountains. A fine scenic path along the edge of the escarpment leads onto Cunswick Fell, and you continue over Kendal Fell before the final descent through the lovely Serpentine Wood into the town centre. There are several climbs on this walk but they are all long and steady rather than steep and strenuous.

The 'Auld Grey Town' of Kendal, so called because of the pale grey colour of the local limestone, lies on the River Kent and is one of the main gateways to the Lake District. In the Middle Ages it was England's pioneer woollen town, renowned for its 'Kendal Green', a course cloth worn by bowmen, and Flemish weavers were allowed to settle here in the 14th century. The large, imposing and unusually wide 13th-century church reflects the prosperity of the medieval woollen industry. Nearby is the Georgian mansion of Abbot Hall, its complex of buildings now housing an art gallery and museum. On the hilltop above the east side of the river are the scanty remains of a 13th-century castle, birthplace of Catherine Parr, sixth and last wife of Henry VIII. Kendal is particularly well known nowadays for Kendal Mint Cake, a recommended accompaniment to long walks on the fells.

Start in front of Kendal Town Hall and take the road opposite, Allhallows Lane. Continue uphill along Beast Banks and, where the road forks, keep ahead along a tarmac path, raised above the road on the left, across the left-hand edge of an open, grassy area. At a crossroads, keep ahead along Brigsteer Road and follow it gently uphill to cross the A591.

After the road curves to the left, you come to the first of two stone stiles and public footpath signs to Scout Scar. Ignore the first of these but at the next one turn right **Ⓐ** over the stone stile and bear slightly left to follow a faint path across an uneven meadow – formerly Kendal racecourse – making for a metal kissing-

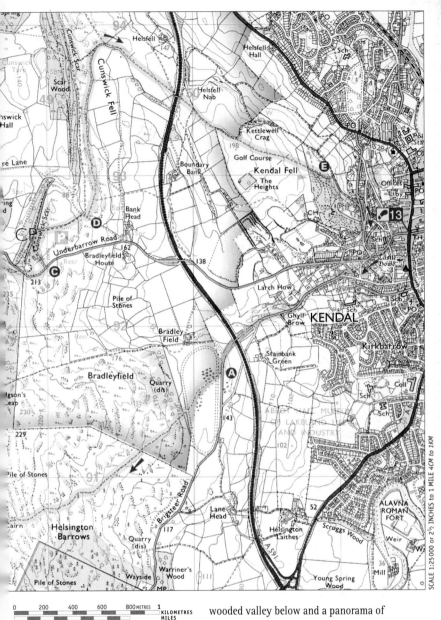

SCALE 1:25000 or 2½ INCHES to 1 MILE 4CM to 1KM

0	200	400	600	800 METRES
0	200	400	600 YARDS	½

KILOMETRES 1
MILES

wooded valley below and a panorama of the Lakeland fells on the horizon.

Turn right at a cairn to follow a path along the top of the escarpment. This is a lovely part of the walk. You then pass below a stone shelter covered by a dome, and eventually the path turns right and descends to go through a metal kissing-gate on to a road. Turn right and at a footpath sign which says 'Permissive Path, Cunswick Fell' turn left along a tarmac track **C**.

gate in the wall on the far side. Go through the gate, keep ahead gently uphill across an area of rough pasture between bushes and fern, climb a stone stile and continue across heathery moorland, following a clear, winding and undulating path to the edge of the escarpment of Scout Scar **B**. From here there is a magnificent view ahead with a well-

View north-west from Scout Scar, near Kendal

Continue into trees. The track now becomes a rough path, which keeps along the right inside edge of woodland, by a wall on the right, to reach a kissing-gate and another 'permissive path' sign. Turn right through a kissing-gate, continue along the left-hand edge of a meadow, by a wall on the left, and in the field corner turn right to continue alongside a wall. At the wall corner, bear left **D**, in the direction of a public footpath sign Cunswick Fell, and head across to another footpath sign. Do not follow its direction to the right but continue past it along a wide, grassy path to a waymarked stile. Climb it, keep ahead, by a wall on the right, and follow the wall as it curves steadily to the right across Cunswick Fell.

Look out for a stone stile in the wall soon after the right-hand curve – it could easily be missed – climb it and continue along the right-hand edge of a field, by a wall on the right. Where the wall curves right, keep straight ahead, descending gently and making for a footbridge over the A591. Climb a ladder-stile on the far side of the field, turn left over the footbridge, climb a stile on the other side

and continue across a field, joining and keeping by a wall on the left. Climb two stone stiles and, where the wall bends left, keep ahead in a straight line across a golf-course on Kendal Fell, later bearing left and making for a stone stile at the left-hand corner of a wood.

Climb the stile, and follow a path slightly to the left to reach some seats, put there in order that people can pause to admire the grand view over Kendal. The path then bears right to keep parallel with a wall bordering the wood and bears right again to enter Serpentine Wood **E**, a beautiful area of woodland and a popular recreational area for the people of the town. Any downhill path through the wood will lead back to the centre of Kendal but, in order to follow the precise route, take the left-hand path at a crossing of paths, continue along the left-hand, lower path at a fork and follow it downhill, via a series of steps, to climb a stone stile at the bottom edge of the woodland onto a track.

Turn right to a road, bear right along it and at a fork take the left-hand, lower road, Serpentine Road. At a T-junction, turn left downhill and follow the road back to the starting point.

Hadrian's Wall and the River Irthing

Start	Birdoswald
Distance	7½ miles (12.1km)
Approximate time	3½ hours
Parking	Birdoswald
Refreshments	Pubs in Gilsland, cafeteria at Birdoswald
Ordnance Survey maps	Landranger 86 (Haltwhistle), Outdoor Leisure 43 (Hadrian's Wall)

The two best sites on Hadrian's Wall within Cumbria are Birdoswald Fort and Milecastle 48. In addition, there are a couple of substantial sections of the wall between them, and this walk along high ground overlooks these sites and the topography in which the Romans built this part of their boundary defences. The walk also encompasses a scenic reach of the River Irthing, which meanders in a deep gorge that formed part of the defences.

Walk up the hill from the car park to the partly excavated remains of Birdoswald, known to the Romans as Camboglanna, a fort measuring 580 by 400ft (177 by 122m), being nearly 5½ acres (2.2ha) in extent and, if fully excavated, might well compete in importance with Housesteads or Chesters. Much of the perimeter defences up to about one course high is well preserved with the foundations of their towers, but little of the internal buildings has been exposed. A farmhouse and outbuildings take up part of the site. However, there is an interpretative centre adjoining the fort with good graphics and models that explain and enhance much of what will be seen on the walk.

From the fort, walk along a fine ⅓-mile (536m) section of wall to Milecastle 49 Ⓐ, which is signed. The milecastle is perched on the very edge of the Irthing gorge, the bridge over which it and the fort were built to defend.

The wall is unusual in having regularly spaced drain holes through it, made necessary by the marshy ground to the south, and for the number of phallic symbols cut in its stones, although it takes a patient eye to find the latter. The milecastle, excavated in 1953, measures 65 by 75ft (20 by 23m), and the layout of the external and internal walls is plain to see. From the castle the wall dropped down to a bridge spanning the river, but there is now no trace apart from massive remains of a former bridge and tower on the further bank, some 100 yds (91m) north of the modern steel footbridge. These remains are detailed on English Heritage boards nearby.

Cross the steel footbridge and walk on in the direction of Gilsland, passing the remains of Turret 48A. Part of the wall on the west side of the turret lies tumbled in the River Irthing, which has encroached on it. Otherwise this section of wall is fourteen courses high.

Go over the road and join a footpath between the school and the car park, where there is information about Willowford and Hadrian's Wall. Finger-posts at the entrance to the footpath direct walkers to Throp Farm and Milecastle 48.

Turn half right in the direction of Throp Farm by walking up a track to the railway embankment. Cross the line with care and climb a stile **B**.

If you wish to visit the Poltross Burn Milecastle 48, take a detour left. Cross a stile and continue beside the railway embankment to a stile and the site of the milecastle. Return to point **B**.

Continue westwards over the ladder-stile across the original path. In the field beyond there is no clear right-of-way through the grass, so just make for the high ground and then scan the stone wall ahead for stone steps let into it. Over the wall, set a course across the next field towards Throp Farm. Again

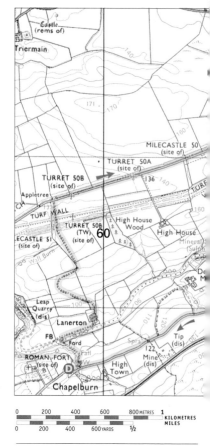

look for steps set in the stone wall round the farm and, when over it, walk

---

The foundations of the Roman bridge at Willowford, looking east

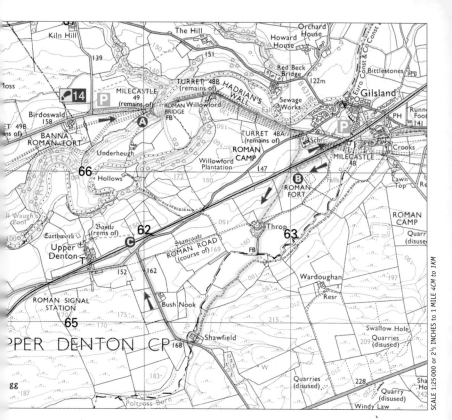

left down a grass lane, through a gate and follow a fence to Poltross Burn to cross the wooden footbridge.

The next stage is to make for Shawfield Farm along the right-of-way, which is none too obvious. Make for the first pole of the electricity cables running across the field and then walk slightly uphill parallel with them. At the far corner of the field, go through a gate and up to near the top of the next field, which will put you on a level grass ledge, leading to the first of two gates into the farmyard, now used as a car-breaker's yard. Coming out of the yard onto the minor road, walk downhill to the right-hand bend and there bear left **C** along the lesser road to Upper Denton, beside which is a charming 9th-century church nestling among the trees in a churchyard full of lopsided gravestones.

From this minuscule village there is a 1½ mile (2.4km) walk along the road westwards with sweeping views across the Irthing valley to the patchwork of fields divided by lines of trees on the opposite slopes, atop which runs Hadrian's Wall. The immediate destination is Chapelburn, where the right-of-way passes down beside a picture-postcard white cottage **D** and across its garden, keeping between two rows of stones laid across the lawn. Leave the garden by a gate into a meadow that sweeps down to the river, aiming at the far, left-hand corner to cross an undulating suspension bridge. Turn right along the far bank in the shade of sycamore trees to Lanerton Farm. After passing through the yard, take the farm road that snakes up the hill to reach the road going east back to Birdoswald, which, incidentally, is part of the Cumbria Cycle Way and closely follows the line of Hadrian's Wall, fragments of which occasionally appear beside the road. ●

Ullswater

Start	Pooley Bridge
Distance	6½ miles (10.5km)
Approximate time	3¼ hours
Parking	Pooley Bridge
Refreshments	Hotels, pubs and cafés at Pooley Bridge
Ordnance Survey maps	Landranger 90 (Penrith, Keswick & Ambleside), Outdoor Leisure 5 (The English Lakes – North Eastern area)

Ullswater, the second-largest lake in the Lake District, stretches from Pooley Bridge in the north to Patterdale in the south. A typical example of a trough gouged out by glaciation, it is in parts over 200ft (61m) deep. It is best viewed from a height, and there are some particularly satisfying views from the bridleway that climbs to just over 1000ft (305m) along the base of the crags of Barton Fell. These views also encompass the Helvellyn range, lesser heights and a delightful stroll along the lake shore.

Pooley Bridge was once a quiet fishing and farming village, but nowadays it is a busy walking and tourist centre. Leave the village by the riverside path, starting beside the 19th-century stone bridge over the River Eamont. The first part of the lakeside walk is between ancient trees, and, after emerging from them one passes a number of small bays, each with its grey shingle beach, moored boats and little copse on its headland. After nearly 1 mile (1.6km) the path passes through a campsite at Waterside House **Ⓐ**.

Follow the farm road out to the Howtown road, turning right, walk past the first kissing-gate on the left and 100 yds (91m) further on turn up the farm road to Gross Dormont **Ⓑ**. Turn right beside the first white farm building and then left around the back of it to go over a stile and across a field to Seat Farm. Here there is a notice 'No right of way through farmyard' but plenty of signs keep you on the right track. Beyond the farm buildings, go

through a gate on the left and continue on the other side of a stone wall, around two more fields in which a single strand of wire on posts keeps you along the edges, until you come to a jump over a small stream and a gate into Crook-a-dyke.

Keep close to the stone wall on the left until you reach a kissing-gate **Ⓒ** with a signpost to Howtown and Martindale. Go through this gate and follow a trodden way up the fell through gorse and reed-beds. The track wanders a bit, but there are three white-topped marker-posts to follow. From here on, the views over the lake start to become more expansive as you gain height. Soon the gorse is left behind, and the ground becomes boulder-strewn. Make for the east corner of Auterstone Wood **Ⓓ** – the trees are now thin on the ground – and here turn left up the bridleway running above Lock Bank. The escarpment of Auterstone Crag rises impressively above the way, which is stony and slightly rutted. Ullswater and the hills

| 0 | 200 | 400 | 600 | 800 METRES | 1 |
| 0 | 200 | 400 | 600 YARDS | ½ | KILOMETRES MILES |

beyond are impressive from here. One can also look down on the route taken. Barton Park is a dense, mixed broadleaf wood, which for a while blots out Ullswater. Soon after emerging from the wood, the bridle-way drops down into a ravine to Aik Beck, which flows between tumbled boulders. As you walk up the other side, there is a good view down the ravine to the foot of the lake and the wooded, Christmas pudding shape of Dunmallard Hill.

The gradient now levels a bit on the way to the Cockpit, a stone circle of unknown date about 85ft (26m) in internal diameter. It is actually two concentric circles, but this is not obvious, and the stones are unimpressively small.

A number of Bronze Age barrows and cairns are dotted around Askham Fell, immediately east of the Cockpit. From here take the path bearing half-left, and then it is virtually downhill all the way back to Pooley Bridge. After 300 yds (274m), turn left again down a wide bridleway at the crossroads **E**, marked by a cairn and four-fingered signpost. The bridleway runs fairly steeply down to a gate by the driveway to Roehead. Through the gate, it becomes a metalled road running into Pooley Bridge, beside the church. Walk through the village to the bridge, from where there is a lovely view up the river and the length of Ullswater. For one last look at the lake, walk a further 400 yds (366m) to the steamer pier. From the end you see the whole walk along the opposite shore and up the fellside. ●

Low Furness

Start	Furness Abbey
Distance	7½ miles (12.1km). Shorter version 4½ miles (7.2km)
Approximate time	3½ hours (2 hours for shorter version)
Parking	Amphitheatre car park on south side of Furness Abbey
Refreshments	Pub by Furness Abbey, pubs at Newton, pubs and café at Dalton-in-Furness
Ordnance Survey maps	Landranger 96 (Barrow-in-Furness & South Lakeland), Outdoor Leisure 6 (The English Lakes – South Western area)

Furness literally means 'far ness', and this formerly inaccessible area comprises the fells of High Furness, part of the Lake District National Park, and the peninsula of Low Furness, a region of green, rolling hills and shallow valleys. This walk explores part of the latter region: starting at one of the foremost monastic sites in the country, passing through three hamlets, visiting the medieval capital of Furness (Dalton-in-Furness) and finishing off with a walk through the lovely wooded Vale of Nightshade. Furness was an important source of iron ore, hence the sudden rise of Barrow in the 19th century, but there is little evidence of this industrial heritage on this peaceful walk, except for some abandoned iron mines and views over Barrow shipyards and Walney Channel. There may be cattle on some pastures passed through. The shorter version omits two of the three hamlets.

The extensive and well-preserved red sandstone ruins of Furness Abbey occupy such a peaceful and beautiful setting in the well-wooded Vale of Nightshade that it is difficult to believe Barrow lies just over the next hill. Founded in 1127, the abbey rapidly grew into one of the wealthiest Cistercian monasteries in England and, in this far flung region well away from the main centres of power, the abbots of Furness exercised almost quasi-monarchic powers. Its wealth was based on sheep farming, quarrying and iron-mining on its extensive estates, though it was subject to Scottish sea-borne raids

from time to time. The transepts and east end of the church are almost complete, as is the east range of the cloisters, the latter noted for the flamboyant, decorative Norman arches that lead into the 13th-century chapter-house. Furness suffered the same fate as all the other great abbeys and was dissolved on the orders of Henry VIII in 1537.

Start by turning right along the lane and after about 50 yds (45m) turn right along a path through trees, which soon becomes a tarmac path enclosed by iron fencing. Cross a railway line, go through a metal kissing-gate and bear right to walk along the right-hand edge of a field, soon joining and keeping by Mill Beck on the right, up to the attractive Bow Bridge. This is thought to date from the 15th century and was one of the links in the large number of routes that radiated from the abbey at the height of its power.

Go through a metal kissing-gate onto a road, turn left beneath an avenue of trees and turn right by a road junction **A** through a metal kissing-gate, by a public footpath sign to Newton. Follow the direction of the signpost uphill across rough pasture to a waymarked post, where you pass through a wall gap and continue uphill, by a hedge on the left. Where the hedge peters out, keep ahead to a metal kissing-gate **B**, and ahead are the houses of Newton.

For the shorter version of the walk, go through the gate, head gently downhill along the right-hand edge of a field, by a hedge on the right, and go through another metal kissing-gate onto a lane on the edge of Newton. Continue along the lane opposite, bearing first right and then left, follow it through the village and at a public footpath sign to Long Lane turn left onto a tarmac track, here rejoining the full walk.

For the full walk, do not go through the gate but turn right to keep along the top edge of the field, by a fence and hedge on the left, to a stile. From here there are views over Barrow and Walney Channel, and out in the channel Piel Castle, owned by the medieval abbots of Furness, can be seen. Climb the stile, continue along the top edge of the next field, made uneven by the remains of disused iron mines, and turn left over a ladder-stile, just before reaching the brow of the hill in front. Bear right and head diagonally across a field; note that there is no visible path here. Make for a metal kissing-gate, go through this and continue on to a lane and turn right downhill into the hamlet of Stank.

Just before reaching farm buildings, turn left **C** through a metal gate along a track to a footpath sign and turn right around the end of a barn. Climb a stile, bear slightly left and head across to a waymarked post to the left of a barn. Continue past it to the field corner and turn left to walk along the right-hand edge of the field, by a hedge on the right. Climb a stile a few yards to the left of the field corner, keep along the left edge of the next field for a short distance and then climb a stile in the hedge on the left to continue uphill, now along the right edge of a field, by a hedge on the right. Over the brow, a fine view across Furness is revealed, with the outline of the Lakeland mountains to the left. Descend into a 'dip', climb a stile in the field corner, turn right along the bottom edge of the next field and turn left in the field corner to continue uphill along the right-hand edge of the field. In the top corner, climb a stile and keep ahead across the next field, heading downhill in the direction of Dendron church, to go through a metal gate in the bottom right-hand corner.

Walk through a farmyard, follow a track to right and left and continue down to a lane **D** just to the left of Dendron's 17th-century church, one of the few to be built during the Civil War. Turn left along the lane for nearly ³/₄ mile (1.2km), following it around left and right bends, and at a public footpath sign turn left through a metal kissing-gate **E**. Head across a field and turn right on the far side to keep alongside a hedge. Pass through a metal gate into the next field and, on reaching a track, turn left along it. Keep along the right-hand edge of a field, by a hedge on the right – it later becomes an enclosed track – to reach a metal gate. Go through, turn right over a waymarked stile a few yards ahead, bear left and head across a field to a squeezer stile; this may be difficult to spot but it is about 100 yds

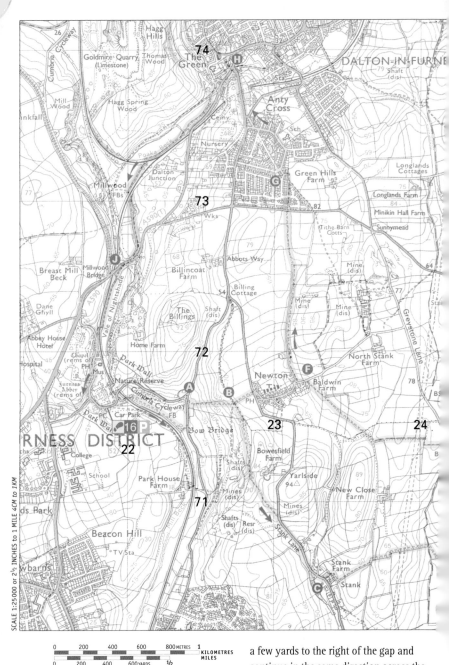

SCALE 1:25000 or 2½ INCHES to 1 MILE 4CM to 1KM

| 0 | 200 | 400 | 600 | 800 METRES | 1 |
| 0 | 200 | 400 | 600 YARDS | ½ |

KILOMETRES
MILES

(91m) to the left of the right-hand field corner.

Go through the stile, continue in the same direction across two fields, going through more squeezer stiles, and bear right after the second one and make for a wide gap in the field corner. Climb a stile

a few yards to the right of the gap and continue in the same direction across the next field, descending to go through a squeezer stile onto a lane (difficult to spot until you are close) **F**. Turn left into Newton and, just before reaching a pub, turn right, at a public footpath sign Long Lane, along a tarmac track, which soon continues as a hedge-lined, enclosed path. Where this path bends right, keep ahead

The red sandstone ruins of Furness Abbey

through a squeezer stile and continue across a succession of fields and through a series of squeezer stiles to emerge onto a road on the edge of Dalton-in-Furness. Cross over, take the tarmac path opposite between new houses, cross another road and continue along a narrow path. Bear left on joining another path and eventually turn left along a track to reach a road, by a public footpath sign North Stank .

Turn right, at a T-junction turn right again and at the next T-junction turn left along a road to another T-junction. Here turn right along the main road and follow it steeply downhill to a junction **H**, where the route continues sharply to the left. Turn right if visiting the centre of Dalton-in-Furness, which was the 'capital' of Furness in the Middle Ages. Around the market square is Dalton Castle, a 14th-century tower in which the abbots of Furness held their courts, some attractive cottages and an ornate Victorian cast-iron fountain in the middle. Nearby is the large, mainly 19th-century church.

After turning left, take the first turning on the right, Goose Green, follow the lane as it curves left and, at a public footpath sign to Millwood, bear right along a tarmac drive. After a few yards, turn left to cross a footbridge over a stream, go through a kissing-gate and continue along a track through the pleasant, well-wooded valley.

The track narrows to a path and continues along the right inside edge of woodland. Go through a metal kissing-gate, continue to go through another and shortly turn left to pass under a railway bridge. Continue to the right, turn left to pass under another railway bridge, turn right, and the path later becomes a hedge- and tree-lined track that heads uphill to a road **J**. Cross over and, at a public footpath sign Furness Abbey, take the path opposite, which bends right and continues through woodland. Emerging from the trees, continue along an enclosed path through the Vale of Nightshade, turn right to pass once more under a railway bridge and turn left to continue to a lane.

Walk along the lane, passing under an arch to the right of the Abbey Tavern and following it past the abbey ruins to return to the start. ●

Dunnerdale Fells

Start	Parking area ¾ mile (1.2km) south of Ulpha Bridge
Distance	6½ miles (10.5km)
Approximate time	3½ hours
Parking	Parking area south of Ulpha Bridge
Refreshments	None
Ordnance Survey maps	Landranger 96 (Barrow-in-Furness & South Lakeland), Outdoor Leisure 6 (The English Lakes – South Western area)

Wordsworth thought the Duddon was the loveliest of rivers and wrote a series of sonnets in praise of it. Both the silvan delights of the Duddon valley and the bare, craggy outlines of the Dunnerdale Fells above it can be appreciated on this walk. It is not a strenuous walk as there are no steep ascents and descents but as this is one of the more remote and less frequented parts of the Lake District, the paths are relatively underused. Therefore, there are some rough and uneven sections and at times, especially on the final descent, the paths are overgrown and in a few places almost obliterated by bracken. Do not let this deter you, however, from enjoying what is a superb walk amidst glorious scenery.

From the car park, turn right along the road towards Ulpha and just before the road bends left to Ulpha Bridge, turn right **A**, at a public bridleway sign, onto a track that winds steadily uphill to a farm. Keep ahead at a fork along the left-hand track, go through a gate into woodland and continue through the wood to go through another gate on the far side.

At a fork just beyond the gate, take the right-hand uphill track, by a wall on the left, and from it there are grand views looking up the Duddon valley. Follow the track through several gates, descending to pass to the right of farm buildings and finally heading up to reach a narrow lane **B**. Turn right along it, first heading uphill to pass below the summit of Stickle Pike and then descending. Just in front of

a metal gate, turn right **C** up to a public footpath sign and turn left to keep alongside a wall on the left. Follow the wall round to the right to head steeply uphill and at a corner follow the wall round again to the left and continue by it along the side of the valley for ¾ mile (1.2km). The narrow, undulating path is rough, boggy and overgrown by bracken in places. It passes above a farm on the left and finally descends to cross a beck. Immediately turn right for a few yards, then turn left by a wall on the left, go through a metal gate in front and continue along an uphill, grassy track enclosed by broken walls. All around are fine views over rugged fells. Where the walled track ends, turn right between gateposts and head diagonally downhill

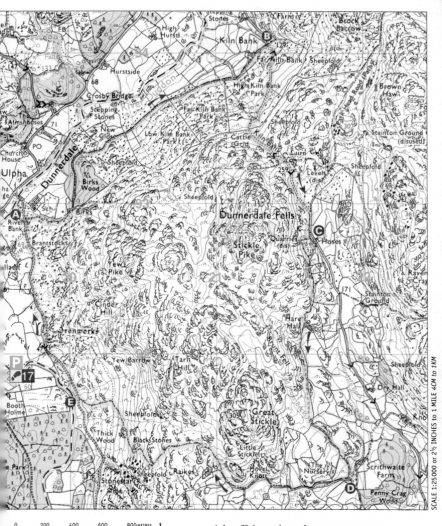

SCALE 1:25000 or 2½ INCHES TO 1 MILE 4CM to 1KM

0	200	400	600	800 METRES	1	
						KILOMETRES
						MILES
0	200	400	600 YARDS	½		

across a field to pass through a gap in the bottom corner.

Here turn sharp right **D** along another enclosed, walled track. As the track heads uphill, superb views open up of the Dunnerdale Fells ahead and the Duddon estuary to the left. Later, descend to go through a gate, keep ahead and, where the enclosed track peters out just before a barn, pass to the right of the barn to head uphill along a grassy path. Go through a gate and bear left to continue by a wall on the left, passing below Great Stickle. Just before reaching a gate on the left, bear

right off the main path onto a narrower path and head steeply uphill between bracken, still keeping parallel to the wall on the left, to reach a fork just on the brow of the hill.

Take the left-hand path that winds downhill between grass and bracken, going around several sharp bends. On this descent there are magnificent views over the Duddon valley, with the winding river and the houses of Ulpha seen below. The path is generally discernible but there are places where it is almost engulfed by bracken and consequently difficult to follow. Eventually, you reach a road at a public bridleway sign **E** and turn right along it for ¼ mile (400m) to the start. ●

Angle Tarn and Hayeswater

Angle Tarn and Hayeswater

Start	Brothers Water. Car park off A592 just beyond north end of lake
Distance	7 miles (11.3km)
Approximate time	3½ hours
Parking	Brothers Water
Refreshments	None
Ordnance Survey maps	Landranger 90 (Penrith, Keswick & Ambleside), Outdoor Leisure 5 (The English Lakes – North Eastern area)

A steady climb from near the shores of Brothers Water leads up to Boredale Hause, a fine viewpoint overlooking Ullswater and the Helvellyn range, and the route continues across empty and austere moorland, passing lonely Angle Tarn, before descending steeply to the foot of Hayeswater. Finally, there comes a pleasant walk beside Hayeswater Gill and through the attractive hamlet of Hartsop to return to the start. There are several moderate ascents and descents and some boggy stretches but the route is generally easy to follow, and from the higher points there are impressive views of the surrounding fells.

Turn right out of the car park along the road, take the first turning on the left, signposted Hartsop, and turn left just past a house **Ⓐ**, at a public bridleway sign, along a straight tarmac track. This later becomes a rough track that keeps below steep fells on the right. Go through a gate, cross a footbridge over a beck, continue to a fork and here take the right-hand, upper track which climbs steadily, giving fine views of Ullswater and the Helvellyn range.

Climb quite steeply to reach a track and bear right along it to a small cairn **Ⓑ**. This is Boredale Hause, a flat, grassy col, which is the meeting-place of several paths and was once part of a pack-horse trail between Boredale and Patterdale. To the right are the fragmentary remains of a small chapel. Just past the cairn, continue along the right-hand path, which crosses a beck and then winds through rough grass and bracken, climbing steadily all the while and passing several cairns. To the right is a fine view of Brothers Water, framed by high fells. At a fork, continue along the left-hand path, which bends right to pass below Angletarn Pikes and continues on to the lonely and austere Angle Tarn. Pass to the left of the tarn, continue to a gate, go through and follow an undulating path, initially keeping by a broken wall and later a wire fence on the right. The route is partly marked by cairns, and there are superb views to the left down Bannerdale to the line of the Pennines on the horizon.

The path bends right to ford a stream, goes through a gap in a wall and continues by a wire fence on the right.

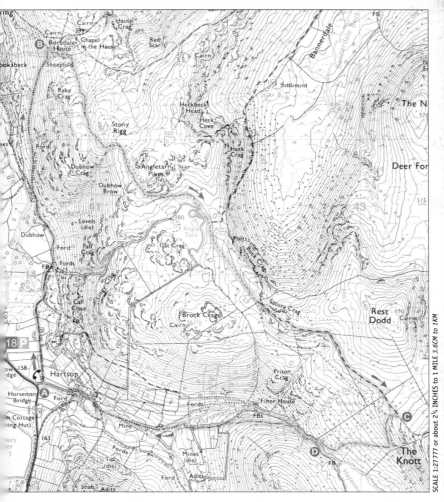

SCALE 1:27777 or about 2¼ INCHES to 1 MILE 3.6CM to 1KM

0	200	400	600	800 METRES	1
					KILOMETRES
					MILES
0	200	400	600 YARDS	½	

Later, leave the fence and keep ahead across a boggy area, go through a gap in a wall and continue uphill across the lower slopes of the Knott – the conical hill directly in front – to reach a T-junction of paths by a cairn just below the summit **C**.

Turn right, and ahead is a majestic view of the Helvellyn range on the skyline with Hayeswater, Brothers Water and the valley of Hayeswater Gill below. Head downhill, bending right above Hayeswater and later curving left to continue quite steeply down to the end of the lake. Cross a footbridge over a stream at the foot of Hayeswater **D** and shortly turn left along a clear track that descends above rocky Hayeswater Gill.

Go through a kissing-gate, continue downhill, turn right to cross a footbridge over the beck and turn left to keep along the other side of it. Go through a gate, continue along a tarmac track that descends gently to a kissing-gate, go through this and walk through a car park and along a lane through the hamlet of Hartsop, which has some attractive 17th-century farm buildings and a few cottages that retain their old spinning-galleries. After passing through the hamlet, you rejoin the outward route and retrace your steps back to the starting point.

River Lowther and Shap Abbey

Start	Shap
Distance	5½ miles (8.9km)
Approximate time	3 hours
Parking	Shap
Refreshments	Pubs and cafés at Shap
Ordnance Survey maps	Landranger 90 (Penrith, Keswick & Ambleside), Outdoor Leisure 5 (The English Lakes – North Eastern area)

From Shap village the route heads across an austere limestone landscape of fields and drystone walls to descend into the Lowther valley. It then continues through the valley, following part of the Coast-to-Coast Walk, to the attractively sited ruins of Shap Abbey and on to the hamlet of Keld. From here field paths lead back to the start. This is an undemanding walk, with no strenuous or particularly difficult sections, and there are many fine and uninterrupted views to the west and south over bleak and empty moorlands.

Shap was once notorious for the heavy traffic that thundered through it on the A6 and for vehicles being stranded in wintry weather on the bleak Shap Fells to the south, but since the construction of the M6 it has become a quiet backwater. The many inns lining the main street are evidence of its former traffic, and near the start of the walk is an attractive 17th-century market cross.

Turn right out of the car park through the village and turn left along a lane signposted to Bampton and Haweswater. Shortly after a left-hand bend, turn right through a metal gate Ⓐ, at a public footpath sign Rosgill, and head diagonally across a large field, making for a gate in the far corner. Go through, keep in the same direction across the next field, climb a ladder-stile and head diagonally across

the next field to climb a stone stile onto a lane.

Turn right and, at a public footpath sign, turn left Ⓑ over a stone stile and walk diagonally across a rather rough and uneven field to climb a stile in the corner. Bear slightly right along the left-hand edge of the next field, by a wall on the left. Where the wall bears left, keep straight ahead to climb a stone stile in the wall in front. From here there is a grand view ahead over the fells. Continue in the same direction across a series of fields and over a succession of stone stiles, eventually reaching a waymarked gate. Go through it, bear slightly right across a field to climb a stone stile by a wall corner and continue along the left-hand edge of the field, by a wall and wire fence on the left. Climb another stone stile and keep

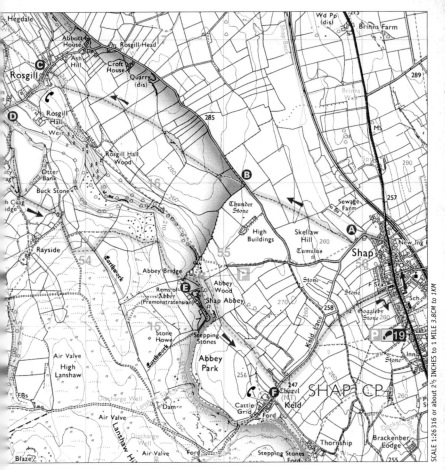

SCALE 1:26316 or about 2½ INCHES to 1 MILE 3.8CM to 1KM

ahead over one more onto a lane in the hamlet of Rosgill **C**.

Turn left down the lane, cross a bridge over the River Lowther and shortly afterwards, where the lane bends right, turn left over a stile, at a public footpath sign Coast to Coast **D**. Walk along a track, by a wall on the right, and follow it as it curves right to go through a metal gate. Now bear left off the track to continue beside a wall on the left, climb a stone stile, at a public footpath sign Shap Abbey, and continue by a wall – later a wire fence – on the left along the bottom edge of sloping meadows. Turn left to cross the picturesque old Parish Crag Bridge over Swindale Beck, head uphill, by a wire fence on the left, and continue across a field to climb a ladder-stile on the far side. Keep ahead to climb another and

turn right along a tarmac track.

At a public footpath sign to Shap, turn left and head across rough, boggy pasture, veering right from the wall on the left, to a stile. Climb it and continue along the right-hand edge of a field, by a wall on the right. Where the wall ends, turn right along a faint but discernible path. Veer left away from the wall on the right, descend to rejoin it and follow the wall along to a ladder-stile. Climb it, turn half-right and head across a sloping meadow above the river towards the ruins of Shap Abbey. Bear slightly right to climb a ladder-stile above Abbey Bridge and drop down to a track. Turn right to visit the abbey but otherwise turn left to cross the footbridge over the River Lowther 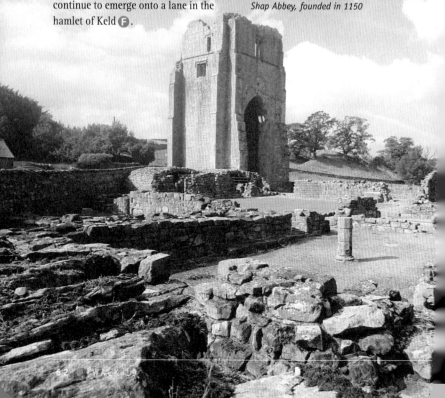.

Shap Abbey was founded towards the end of the 12th century by monks of the Premonstratensian Order and occupies a most attractive position amidst lonely fells beside the river. The main surviving portion is the impressive west tower, built about 1500 and standing almost to its full height.

After crossing the bridge, walk along the track ahead to a T-junction. Keep ahead along an uphill path, at the top of the rise turn right to a stone stile, climb it and continue along the right-hand edge of a field, by a wall and wire fence on the right. Over to the right are impressive views of Shap Abbey below and the wild and desolate moorlands on the other side of the River Lowther. Climb a stone stile and keep ahead across a long, narrow field, parallel to a wall on the left. Look out for a stone stile in that wall, climb it and turn right to continue, now with the wall on the right. Where the wall turns right, keep ahead to pick up and keep by a wall on the left, climb a stile and continue to emerge onto a lane in the hamlet of Keld .

A short distance to the right is a small, 15th-century chapel, probably built by the monks of Shap Abbey for the local people. It is now owned by the National Trust. At one time it was used as a cottage. The route continues to the left up the lane, but after a few yards climb a stone stile in the wall on the right, at a public footpath sign to Shap, and turn left to continue along the left-hand edge of a field, by a wall on the left, parallel to the lane. Climb a stone stile, continue and, where the wall curves left, keep ahead to another stone stile. Climb this, keep ahead to climb another, cross a track, climb the stone stile opposite and continue along the edge of fields, climbing several more stone stiles, until you go over a small rise, and ahead is the village of Shap.

Descend gently, go through a gate and continue between walls to go through another gate onto a track. Turn right, take the first turning on the left to walk through a new housing area and at the main road turn right to return to the start.

Shap Abbey, founded in 1150

Mallerstang and Pendragon Castle

Start	Aisgill Moor Cottages on the North Yorkshire-Cumbria border
Distance	9 miles (14.5km). Shorter version 6 miles (9.7km)
Approximate time	4½ hours (3 hours for shorter version)
Parking	Beside road at Aisgill Moor Cottages
Refreshments	Café at Aisgill Crafts
Ordnance Survey maps	Landrangers 91 (Appleby-in-Westmorland) and 98 (Wensleydale), Outdoor Leisure 19 (Howgill Fells and Upper Eden Valley)

The Mallerstang pass is the gateway into the Vale of Eden and the remotest and probably the least visited place in Cumbria. It starts at the border with North Yorkshire, at the highest point on the Settle–Carlisle railway line. Built in six years by 6000 Welsh and Irish navvies, hundreds of whom died, it was the last major engineering work completed by human muscle alone. With the escarpment of Mallerstang Edge on its east flank and the brooding scars of Wild Boar Fell on the west, the pass is the most dramatic section of this scenic line. Apart from a short uphill stretch at the start, this is an easy walk, but there are likely to be some muddy patches on the Highway and beside the River Eden. The shorter version omits the detour to Pendragon Castle.

Aisgill Moor Cottages were built in the middle of the 19th century to house Midland Railway maintenance staff. A farm road leads over the railway bridge beside the cottages and climbs the fell, after passing the semi-circular Helgill Force to Helgill Farm, and then alongside Hell Gill Gorge, where Hell Gill Beck has eaten deep into the limestone. At Hell Gill Bridge the path joins the Highway **A**, also known as the Roman Road and Old Road on the map. It is the way along which Lady Anne Clifford was carried on her litter to inspect the castles of Pendragon, Brough, Appleby and

Brougham in the Vale of Eden, which she had just inherited at the age of sixty. That was in the mid 17th century, before the road in the valley was built.

Leaving the bridge to your right, walk north along the Highway, which is a broad grass track keeping roughly to the 1410ft (430m) contour. On the right the fell rises steeply, while on the left you can see up and down the valley, threaded by road, railway and river, beyond which is Wild Boar Fell with its rim of rock scars. This pleasant high-level stroll ends after 2 miles (3.2km), where it drops down the fell to the road by the Thrang **B**. On the

Aisgill Viaduct, Mallerstang Dale

Michael Faraday. From here there are two alternative routes to Pendragon Castle. Continue either along the road or return to Shoregill, a tiny hamlet of gentrified cottages, and then along a footpath above the river to Castle Bridge . Pendragon Castle is every romantic's idea of a ruin, small and picturesque, peeping out among trees atop a knoll, surrounded by a now dry moat. Legend has it that it is named after Uther Pendragon, father of King Arthur. The existing remains date from the 12th century, and one of its owners was Hugh de Morville, one of the three knights who murdered Thomas à Becket in 1170. Twice burned down by border Scots, Lady Anne Clifford restored the castle for the last time in 1660. Access is permitted through the gate by the roadside.

way down it crosses several little gills, which make it wet, slippery and quite difficult underfoot.

The Thrang is a small hotel, which was once a Victorian rectory. Just before reaching it, turn left through a gate, at a public footpath sign to Deepgill, and follow a winding track down to a stone bridge over the River Eden ●.

At this point the shorter version of the walk continues ahead along the track.

For the full walk, turn right alongside the river after crossing the bridge, climb a stile and stay by the river to Mallerstang Dairy Farm. Walk through the farm and on through a wood towards Shoregill. Cross a wooden bridge ● on your right just before Shoregill, then turn left and follow a path diagonally across fields to Mallerstang church. Lady Anne Clifford restored this little 14th-century building in 1663, and her coat of arms is prominent inside. Next to the door are shelves from which an 18th-century charity distributed bread – and still does. Many of the navvies killed building the railway are buried without trace in the churchyard.

Outhgill, but a step away, is a cluster of pretty houses, one of which was the home of the village smith and father of scientist

Retrace your steps, either by the road or the riverside path, to Shoregill ● and then along the river to Thrang Bridge ● to rejoin the shorter route. At the bridge, turn right along the track and, on meeting a wall on the right, turn left, fording a stream, and walk across the field to a stone stile. Climb it and keep ahead across several fields and over a number of stiles, eventually going through a gate in a field corner and keeping by a wall on the right to reach a farm track. Turn left along it, cross the river, go through a metal gate and continue to the road ●.

Turn right to follow the road back to Aisgill Moor Cottages – about $2\frac{1}{4}$ miles (3.6km). At Aisgill Farm a detour can be made by going under a railway viaduct on the right to visit the waterfalls ●. ●

Black Combe

Start	Silecroft
Distance	5½ miles (8.9km)
Approximate time	3 hours
Parking	Layby on edge of Silecroft just to the south of the junction of the A595 and A5093
Refreshments	Pub about 200 yds (183m) north of start, pub at Silecroft
Ordnance Survey maps	Landranger 96 (Barrow-in-Furness & South Lakeland), Outdoor Leisure 6 (English Lakes – South Western area)

Rising abruptly from the Irish Sea, Black Combe is an isolated hill in the south-western extremity of the Lake District National Park. Wainwright describes the bridleway that climbs from Whicham to its 1970ft (600m) summit as 'among the most delectable of Lakeland fell paths' and asks: 'Which other can be ascended in carpet slippers?' It is certainly a fine path scenically because although Black Combe itself is rather featureless, its coastal position gives it unrivalled and unimpeded views both inland over the fells and along the coast. Although the route is easy and the climb a steady one along a clear and broad path all the way, boots or strong shoes are still preferable to carpet slippers, and this walk is not recommended in misty weather.

Looking towards Bootle Fell from Black Combe

Begin by turning right along the road towards Silecroft and, at a public footpath sign to Whicham Church and Black Combe, turn left through a kissing-gate. With a grand view of Black Combe in front, walk across a field, crossing a footbridge over a stream near the far end, keep ahead onto a track and turn left along the enclosed track to a road **A**.

Cross over, climb a waymarked stile a few yards ahead, turn right through a metal gate and head diagonally across a field to climb a stile in the top corner. Continue in the same direction across the next field, climb a stile in the far corner and turn left along a tarmac drive. Where the drive turns left to a large white house, keep ahead along an enclosed track, follow it around a left-hand bend and just after passing between redundant gateposts, turn right **B** onto an uphill path to a stile beside a metal gate.

Climb it onto the open fell and now follow a steadily ascending broad path that cuts a green swathe between bracken – higher up it continues between rough grass and heather – for 1¾ miles (2.8km) to the summit of Black Combe. After a fairly steep initial section, the rest of the route is a steady and easy climb. At a fork, you bear right off the main path to reach the summit **C**, which is marked by a triangulation pillar. From here there are magnificent views over the Lakeland fells and Cumbrian coast, and on a clear day the Isle of Man and the Mountains of Mourne in Northern Ireland can be seen.

Retrace your steps from the summit. On the descent there are more fine views to be enjoyed, looking over Whicham, Silecroft, the Cumbrian coast, Duddon estuary and Walney Island.

Rosthwaite, Watendlath and Stonethwaite

Start	Rosthwaite
Distance	5 miles (8km)
Approximate time	4 hours
Parking	National Trust car park, Rosthwaite
Refreshments	Pub and cafés at Rosthwaite and Stonethwaite, tearoom at Watendlath
Ordnance Survey maps	Landranger 90 (Penrith, Keswick & Ambleside), Outdoor Leisure 4 (The English Lakes North Western area)

With the wandering River Derwent, steep and well-wooded craggy sides and a skyline of high fell tops, Borrowdale is one of the acknowledged areas of exceptional beauty in the Lake District. Hugh Walpole made it the setting for his historical sequence beginning with Rogue Herries *(1930). Its villages are much as they always were: small, slate-grey or white-washed, picturesque and tucked away beneath towering hills. Watendlath was once a remote farming hamlet in a hanging valley high above Borrowdale, as isolated as any hamlet could be. Despite its popularity, it still has charm and, outside the high holiday season, is quite magical. Beyond the village is a near-wilderness of rock and bog, designated an important wetland, traversed by a path which at times verges on being a scramble and involving a steep and difficult descent. The mountain panoramas on this walk are superb.*

Leaving the lane from the car park at Rosthwaite, turn left on the road and then almost immediately right, following a sign 'Public bridleway Stonethwaite and Watendlath'. Cross the bridge and at the fork take the left-hand, stony path Ⓐ, which bends round in front of Hazel Bank Hotel and starts climbing up the fell through oak, ash, birch and chestnut. Soon after leaving the tree-line, a gate across the path provides a good place to stop and look back down on Rosthwaite, a cluster of houses nestling against the dark mass of Johnny Wood, and the sharp-pointed, tree-clad Castle Crag over to the right, backed by the rock and screes of Goat Crag. Further on, the path becomes steeper, rough, rutted and obstructed with boulders. But looking back at about 1000ft (305m) the scene has opened out with the Jaws of Borrowdale in view, and the main valley running on to Longthwaite, Seatoller and the Honister Pass and, to the south, Glaramara. The climb eventually ends on the ridge above Watendlath valley, and a gentle slope leads down to the hamlet.

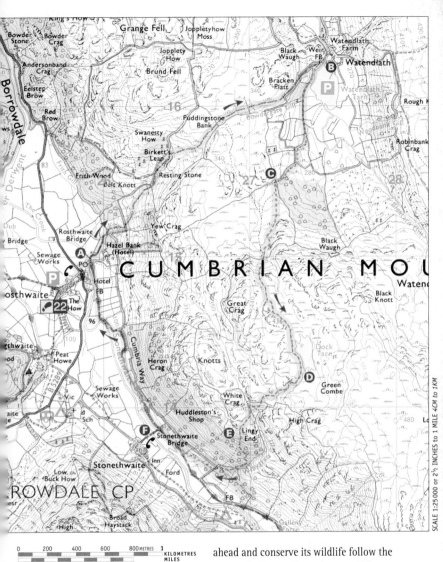

SCALE 1:25000 or 2½ INCHES to 1 MILE 4CM to 1KM

0	200	400	600	800 METRES	1		
						KILOMETRES	
						MILES	
0	200	400	600 YARDS		½		

Watendlath is a pleasant place to
wander around, with its little beck
gurgling out of the tarn under an old
hump-backed, pack-horse bridge. Beside
the water, at the end of the bridleway
from Rosthwaite, a signpost **B** points to
the next destination – Dock Tarn. This
path soon leaves the water's edge,
becoming rough as it rises and crosses
a couple of streams to another sign **C**,
pointing right to Puddingstone Banks and
Rosthwaite and left to Dock Tarn. A notice
states 'To avoid damage to wetland areas

ahead and conserve its wildlife follow the
waymarked route shown by posts'. These
posts are green-topped and augment the
occasional small arrow stuck in the
ground. For a time the going through
squelchy bog would be difficult but for a
number of rocks set down as stepping-
stones. After arriving at a gate, the walk
becomes a climb, almost a scramble, up
Skiddaw slate, where most walkers will
use a few steadying handholds. After
about 100ft (30m) the ground flattens out,
and the route again traverses bog, with
rocks serving as stepping-stones in the
worst parts.

Dock Tarn sits in a shallow basin,

surrounded by blanket bog, little hillocks and outcrops. It is dotted with water lilies and attracts pied wagtails in summer. There is a little beach just off the path. The way round the tarn uses a narrow rock shelf several feet above the water, after which it bears right **D** and starts descending a broad slope, keeping company with Willygrass Gill. It is rough but easy-going until Lingy End, where there is a ruined stone bothy **E**. Pause for the magnificent view of the conjunction of the two deep valleys of Langstrath and Greenup Gill, separated by the great spur of Eagle Crag with its eleven climbs, all for the highly experienced only.

The vertiginous descent into Borrowdale is in parts a 1:3 gradient rock path through a forest of sessile oaks. Although often referred to as steps, the rocks are far from uniform in size or shape, so it is difficult to set a rhythm. Be careful and take your time. Coming out at the bottom of the forest, turn right along a broad track beside a stone wall and follow it all the way back to Rosthwaite. On the way, a diversion can be made over the bridge **F** into Stonethwaite, a tiny village with a café, post office, a few cottages and a hotel with public bar.

Eagle Crag and Langstrath from Lingy End

Carrock Fell and High Pike

Start	Carrock Beck ford over Pasture Lane, ¾ mile (1.2km) south of Calebreck
Distance	7¼ miles (11.7km). Shorter version 5 miles (8km)
Approximate time	3¾ hours (2½ hours for shorter version)
Parking	On grass by ford
Refreshments	None
Ordnance Survey maps	Landranger 90 (Penrith, Keswick & Ambleside), Pathfinder 576, NY 23/33 (Caldbeck)

Carrock Fell is the most easterly of the northern Lakeland hills and is different from its softly rounded, grass-carpeted neighbours in having bouldery slopes, screes and an abrupt escarpment at its eastern end with a rock-strewn base. The escarpment looks over the wide, fertile plain of the Eden valley and is a popular launch site for paragliders. It is also a mecca for amateur geologists because of its variety of interesting rocks and minerals. Both Carrock Fell and its neighbour, Caldbeck Fell, have been heavily mined over the centuries for copper, lead, wolfram and barytes, amongst other minerals, and many people walk these fells for the rather untidy remains of the now disused mines. Great care needs to be taken to avoid old mine shafts that have not been filled in, and it is dangerous to try to enter mine galleries. There is a relatively easy route up and down Carrock Fell, which is crowned by the tumbled walls of a formidable hill fort, but because the summit ridge has no marked path, patches of blanket bog and steep sides to the east and south, it should not be attempted in misty conditions.

A good starting point from which to climb Carrock Fell is where Carrock Beck crosses Pasture Lane, a beauty spot with boulder-strewn ravines on either side. From here it is only a 1300ft (396m) climb to the 2174ft (663m) summit. About 100 yds (91m) up the road from the ford, take the rough mine road on the left **A**, which runs parallel with the beck. Weasel Hills and West Fell, which are part of Caldbeck Fells, rise on your right, and the summit ridge of Carrock Fell keeps you company

1 mile (1.6km) off to the left. After ½ mile (800m) the track rises slightly to meet the bridleway coming from Calebreck and then, after another ½ mile (800m), turn down a grass path that winds away to the left **B** to Carrock Beck. Not well defined and easily missed, it runs alongside the beck for some time before petering out without leading to an obvious crossing point. Just after a minuscule waterfall, look for a grass track going up the opposite bank, where it is possible to take

a long step over the water. This grass track, known as Red Gate, bends first left and then right to climb the fell diagonally in a deep trench, the sides of which are above head height for a long way. When the trench becomes shallower, you can look down and across to the scars and spoil-heaps of Driggeth lead mine 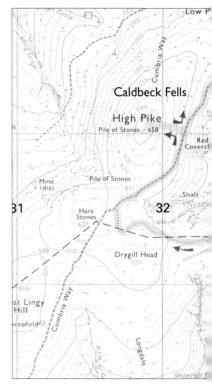, one of three at the head of Carrock Beck. They are three natural ravines down the east face of High Pike, which now look like elongated quarries.

Eventually Red Gate breasts the summit ridge and meets a path coming from the Cumbrian Way, just before it passes below the top of High Pike. Turn left, and it is 1 mile (1.6km) along the ridge to the summit and fort **D** of Carrock Fell. There is no acknowledged path, but a way has been trodden. First comes the pile of stone on top of Miton Hill, no more than a slight rise, then a small cairn. The large summit cairn above the scree and tumbled fort walls can be seen straight ahead. Straight ahead is also the correct route to take to avoid Round Knott, which would involve crossing some bog. Getting into the fort requires the easiest of scrambles up through fallen rocks, and around the

East Pike Cairn, Carrock Fell and the Vale of Eden

summit cairn there is enough protruding rock to give shelter from whichever direction the wind may be blowing. The whole ridge is a viewing-platform for the backs of Skiddaw, Skiddaw Little Man, Blencathra and Bowscale Fell and a peep into its little tarn, entrapped high up on its flank. Beyond these neighbouring hills,

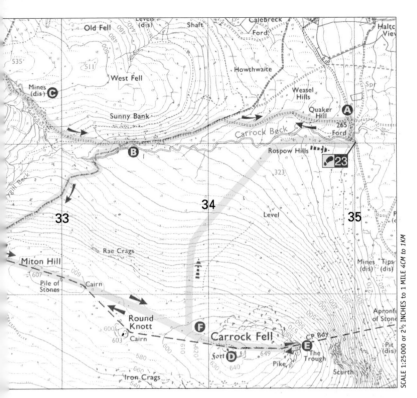

SCALE 1:25 000 or 2½ INCHES to 1 MILE 4CM to 1KM

innumerable high fells and peaks jostle for space across the horizon, some of them more than 15 miles (24km) away. For an altogether different panorama, walk through the fort, down a dip past a substantially built stone shelter and up to the east peak **E** above the escarpment of the fell. Almost the whole of the Eden valley lies at your feet, walled in on its far side by the north Pennines, with Cross Fell centre stage. The valley is a pattern of fertile fields, marked out with bushes and trees, not stone walls, and a network of little roads winds about joining farms, each farm snug in its own windbreak of trees. Turn your head to the left, and there is the Solway Plain and the low hills of Dumfriesshire beyond.

A quick way back to the start is to return the way you came to just beyond the scree surrounding the summit, then turn right **F** *and go straight down the fellside. It is covered with grass all the way, dropping in a series of ridges. On the final ridge, a big sheepfold appears down*

near the river. Alter your direction to pass to the right of it and then make for the left of two hillocks (Rospow Hills). Use them to keep above an area of bog, and then make for the edge of the little ravine above Carrock Beck and follow it to the road.

For the full walk, go back to Miton Hill and the top of Red Gate and return the way you came, or alternatively continue on the track ahead which runs above the ravine of Drygill Beck to join the Cumbria Way and cross the flank of High Pike. It is a short walk up a grass slope to its summit for the ultimate view of the Solway Plain and a plan view of the whole of this walk. Rejoin the Cumbria Way and look out for the top of the rough mine road **G** coming up from Driggeth Mine. Turn down the road, follow it through the workings, to where you left it to cross Carrock Beck on your ascent, and retrace your steps to the starting point.

Newlands Horseshoe

Start	Chapel Bridge, ¼ mile (400m) south-west of Little Town
Distance	8½ miles (13.7km)
Approximate time	5½ hours
Parking	Car park by Chapel Bridge
Refreshments	None
Ordnance Survey maps	Landranger 89 (West Cumbria), Outdoor Leisure 4 (The English Lakes – North Western area)

This is one of the finest of ridge walks. It takes in four summits and provides magnificent and ever-changing views over Derwent Water, Borrowdale, Buttermere and the Newlands valley. The walk begins with a steady climb onto the ridge above the western side of Derwent Water and continues along the ridge over Maiden Moor and High Spy, before descending to Dalehead Tarn. Then comes a steep pull to Dale Head (2473ft/753m), a superb viewpoint. After Hindscarth comes a steep and at times quite difficult descent of Scope End. This walk is not recommended in bad, especially misty weather, unless you are experienced in such conditions and able to use a compass.

From the car park, turn right up the lane and on the edge of Little Town turn sharp right up the second access on the right to a gate at a public footpath sign to Cat Bells Ⓐ. Go through and continue along the track that bends sharply left and ascends gently, by a wall on the left. At a fork, take the right-hand, narrower path, uphill – lined by cairns – to reach a crossing of paths at the col between Cat Bells to the left and Maiden Moor to the right Ⓑ.

Turn right to begin a superb ridge walk with magnificent views all the while over Derwent Water and Borrowdale to the left and the Newlands valley to the right. Follow the path uphill, shortly bearing right to reach the summit of Maiden Moor. Continue along the ridge, climbing up to the tall, slim cairn on the summit of High Spy, and from here descend on a rocky

path towards Dalehead Tarn. The path heads down to the banks of a beck Ⓒ.

Follow a path to the right to ford the beck and head up a newly constructed path, passing to the right of the tarn. This is a badly drained and boggy section but there are plenty of large stones. Now comes the most strenuous part of the walk, heading steeply uphill along a good, clear stony path to the summit cairn on Dale Head. Continue along Hindscarth Edge, following a switchback ridge path as far as a fork Ⓓ. On this part of the walk the Honister Pass and Buttermere can be seen to the left. At the fork, take the right-hand, narrower path gently up to the summit of Hindscarth, enjoying more glorious views over the Newlands valley, with Keswick and Derwent Water in the background and Skiddaw on the

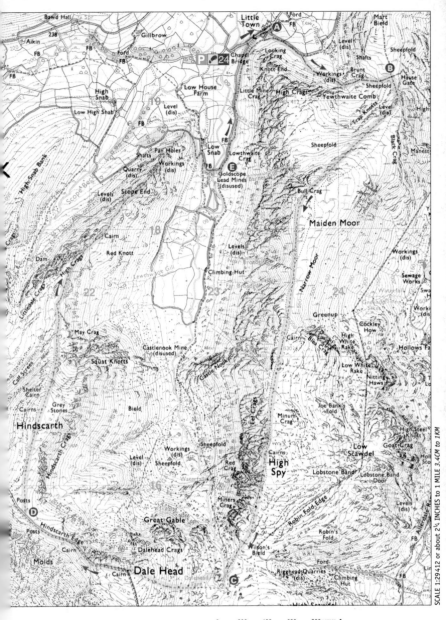

SCALE 1:29412 or about 2¼ INCHES to 1 MILE 3.4M to 1KM

horizon. After passing the summit, the path descends along a narrowing ridge, a steep and quite difficult descent in places, especially the final descent of Scope End.

On reaching a wire fence, follow a path to the right to keep alongside the fence, later curving right away from it to head down to a track just to the right of a farm gate. Turn right along the track. The spoil-heaps ahead are of the Goldscope Mine, worked for about a century from 1565

partly by German miners. Shortly, bear left off the track to follow the wall on the left around to a gate, go through, cross a footbridge over a beck and keep ahead to a track **E**. Turn left and, soon after passing above the car park, look out for a narrow path on the left down to a stile. Climb it and turn left down the lane to the start. ●

0 200 400 600 800 METRES **1**	
	KILOMETRES
	MILES
0 200 400 600 YARDS ½	

Cross Fell

Start	Kirkland
Distance	8½ miles (13.7km)
Approximate time	5 hours
Parking	Layby opposite Kirkland Hall
Refreshments	None
Ordnance Survey maps	Landranger 91 (Appleby-in-Westmorland), Pathfinder 578, NY 62/63 (Appleby-in-Westmorland)

Cross Fell (2930ft/893m) is the highest point on the Pennines, and its broad flat summit makes it look inviting, but its appearance can be deceptive. For six months or more of the year it is a formidable place, taking the full brunt of the weather from all directions. Snow can lie on it well into early summer. Cross Fell's most dreaded feature is the Helm Wind, a local phenomenon, when a band of low cloud sits on it and its neighbouring summits at the same time as a tempestuous wind roars down its west face. It can come without any warning and badly buffets and disorientates the walker. Although more likely to occur in early spring or autumn, the Helm can blow even in July, when the temperature will drop to near freezing. However, when the weather is kind and the air clear, Cross Fell is the finest grandstand in England, with vast views over the Vale of Eden to the Cumbrian Mountains in the west, those of Scotland to the north, and the moorlands of Northumbria spread out to the east and crossed by the valleys of the Tyne and Tees, both rivers born on the eastern slopes of Cross Fell.

Many pass Cross Fell's summit on the Pennine Way walk, but few climb from the Eden valley by the old corpse road and return by a now almost vanished miners' road. It is a satisfying expedition, but one to be attempted only in good weather, unless you are a highly experienced walker able to navigate with a compass.

Kirkland is a tiny cul-de-sac hamlet at the foot of the north Pennines with a glebe farm, a large vicarage and Kirkland Hall. Remarkable are its church and churchyard **Ⓐ**, both far bigger than such

a small place would appear to need. The reason is that Kirkland is at the western end of the corpse road that came over Cross Fell from Garrigill, 9 miles (14.5km) away, where there was no consecrated ground. It is up this corpse road that the walk begins, leaving the village just after Kirkland Hall and climbing and curving up round High Cap. For the first mile (1.6km) the farm road deteriorates into a crumbly, rocky, rutted track. As soon as you gain a little height, the Vale of Eden starts to open up below and remains in

Cross Fell – the Kirkland end of the corpse road

sight until you reach the first disused workings **B**, at the end of a much steeper zigzag section. These were limestone outcrop workings, which now look like a few thousand tons of broken stone bulldozed into a gully. If one looks carefully, there is the suggestion of a building among the rubble, which might have been a shelter for the quarrymen. The ground on the left falls away steeply to Ardale Beck, hurrying down a steep gorge, at the head of which coal was once mined, hence the name Black Doors.

The gradient soon eases a bit, but there is a long slog ahead with many false horizons. The fellside is covered with coarse grass, broken up by great patches of decomposed gritstone. Eventually, a line of small cairns appears ahead as the track nears the point where it joins the Pennine Way, and you turn right **C** towards The Screes, a steep gritstone girdle of tumbled rock round the summit of Cross Fell. The ground is now almost level blanket bog, and in places it is essential to pick a way from one boulder to another. There can be no missing the

point at which the Pennine Way climbs through The Screes as it is where there is a short grassy break in them. Arriving on the east-sloping plateau of the summit, there is a plethora of little cairns, most having no apparent purpose, and neither is there a clear indication of the Pennine Way. Keep going slightly uphill until the triangulation pillar appears and head for it. This is the summit, and beside it is a large stone wind shelter in the form of a cross, giving protection from four points of the compass. At this point, if there is any possibility of a mist coming down or visibility deteriorating for any reason, the less experienced are well advised to retreat down the fell the way they came, which is easy to follow. The route back to the circular walk requires good map and compass work in poor visibility.

To continue the walk, leave the triangulation pillar in a south easterly direction, that is half-left from the direction you came from. Keep on slightly downhill across the summit plateau until you see a single stone **D** standing up like a megalith on the top of The Screes. Make for it, and in its vicinity will be found a gap in The Screes, where it is possible to

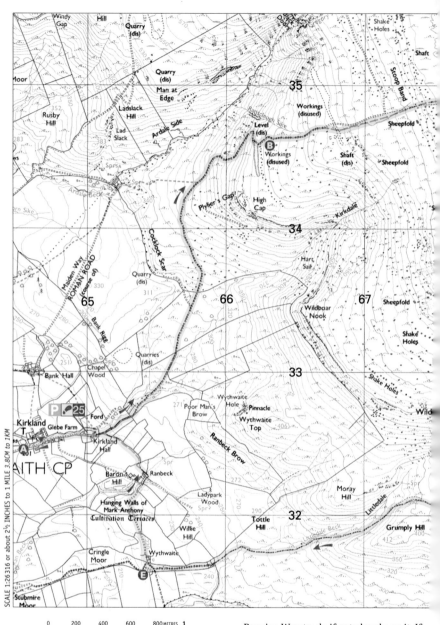

SCALE 1:26316 or about 2½ INCHES to 1 MILE 3.8CM to 1KM

```
0      200    400    600    800 METRES  1
                                         KILOMETRES
                                         MILES
0      200    400    600 YARDS   ½
```

walk down on grass between scattered boulders. To go up or down The Screes requires scrambling. Having reached the more level ground at their base, you may need to adjust your direction to aim at the 'golf ball' of the radar station on the top of Great Dun Fell to the south-east. On this line you should meet the well-worn Pennine Way track, if not already on it. If the 'golf ball' is shrouded in mist, look down the slope ahead of you and aim at a line of concrete slabs that form a path across the boggy ground below. Keep on this track for about 200 yds (183m), when you should meet the bridleway marked on the map coming up from Wythwaite **E**. The leadminers used it to go to work on the other side of Cross Fell, but that was more than 100 years ago, and path is now

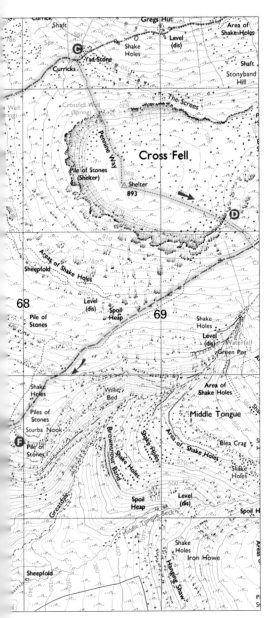

several areas of decomposed gritstone and the spoil-heaps of long-disused lead mines. These lie mostly to your right. On your left is a deep declivity, at the bottom of which flows Crowdundle Beck. It is a desolate ravine and, by keeping well away from its edge, you will be on the right track.

Ahead there is an unusually large cairn **F** (indicated by 'Pile of Stones' on the map), standing on the skyline above Wildboar Scar, which has been in sight most of the way and tends to attract one to it. Ignore it, and keep well to the right towards a much smaller cairn, which marks the start of a narrow path that runs diagonally down the face of the scar. It seems almost too narrow to walk along with its sheer drop on one side, but this is mostly the illusion of vanishing perspective. The path soon reaches the wide grass slopes at the base, from where it is an easy stroll downhill between Grumply Hill and Moray

overgrown or, where visible, no more than a sheep-run.

A number of cairns have been erected over the years along the line of this old bridleway and should be visible if looking south-west. Turn right off the Pennine Way and you will soon either find the merest suggestion of a track to follow or get a sight of the first cairn. After this it is straightforward walking down the side of the fell towards Wildboar Scar, passing

Hill, through two gates to the ruined Wythwaite farmhouse **E**.

Turn right through the yard of the farm, past a more recently built house and onto a metalled road, which runs by way of Ranbeck Farm back to Kirkland. On the way you pass the Hanging Walls of Mark Anthony, ancient cultivation terraces now grass-covered and under a preservation order. They are said to date back to Roman times.

Skiddaw

Start	Gale Road above Latrigg, Keswick
Distance	8 miles (12.9km). Shorter version 5½ miles (8.9km)
Approximate time	5 hours (3 hours for shorter version)
Parking	Car park at end of Gale Road
Refreshments	Hotels at Millbeck and Applethwaite, cottage teas at Millbeck
Ordnance Survey maps	Landranger 90 (Penrith & Keswick), Outdoor Leisure 4 (The English Lakes – North West area)

Skiddaw is the oldest mountain in the Lake District, and at 3053 feet (931m) is one of only four that rise above the 3000ft (914m) height. Surrounded by a group of only slightly lesser heights, it forms a formidable massif, standing isolated from the rest of Lakeland's mountains to dominate the north-west of the region. Well-clothed almost to the very summit in grass and heather with only a few minor strips of scree, this massif has a soft and welcoming look, and the route to the summit from the top of Latrigg is popular. The path presents few dangers, but there are some steep climbs. The shorter version avoids the steep descent by returning the same way. This walk should not be attempted in bad weather unless you are experienced in such conditions and able to navigate by using a compass.

Standing in the car park at the end of Gale Road from Applethwaite, you are already 1000ft (305m) on your way to the top, and looking up you can see the first third of the climb. This is the steepest section of the walk and will occupy about half the time it takes to reach the top. The rounded summit seen from here is that of Little Man, 216ft (66m) below the top of Skiddaw, which is hidden behind it. The sign at the top end of the car park says 'Bridleway to Skiddaw, Millbeck, Bassenthwaite'. Go over a stile, along a neat path of stone-chippings, through a kissing-gate, on past a memorial cross to three shepherds and then down a grass slope to the bottom of the track proper.

The steep gradient along this well-worn route soon gives a line of sight over Keswick, Portinscale, Braithwaite and the north side of Derwent Water, with Cat Bells prominent on the other side of the lake. Behind is a plethora of fells and mountains, and this scene becomes more expansive as one makes for the foot of Little Man, which then obscures everything to the south and west. The twin tops of Little Man first appear soon after the fence, which has kept the path company above White Beck ravine, bears away to the right onto Lonscale Fell while the summit route bears left **A**. The

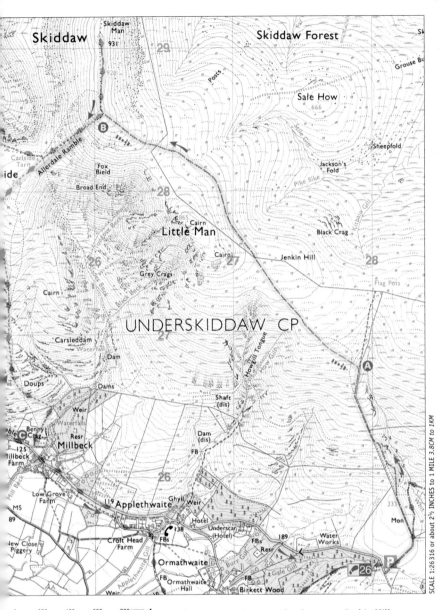

| 0 | 200 | 400 | 600 | 800 METRES | 1 |
| 0 | 200 | 400 | 600 YARDS | ½ | KILOMETRES MILES |

gradient lessens a little until another fence crosses the path and climbs along the side of Little Man. From here on, it is a gentle stroll all the way to the foot of the Skiddaw summit ridge, which is now coming into sight. On the way, it is worth making the effort to climb the short path to the shoulder between the summits of Little Man for an incomparable view of Bassenthwaite Lake. Once past Jenkin Hill the scene to the north and east changes completely. Skiddaw Forest, now all grass, falls away towards Caldbeck Fells, and an isolated lozenge of trees at the foot of a ravine, carrying Salehow Beck, forms an embracing windbreak around the Skiddaw House Youth Hostel.

There is one last climb of 200ft (61m) up the scree side of the Skiddaw ridge to the cairn marking South Top **B**, from where it is about ¼ mile (400m) along the ridge to the true summit, or Skiddaw Man, at 3053ft (931m), where there is a view indicator. The summit is bare and stony, often lashed by winds and decidedly colder than the fellside leading to it. Return to the cairn at South Top, where a decision has to be made.

All but intrepid or hardened fellwalkers are likely to be daunted at the thought of descending the steep scree down to the col of Carl Side. If in doubt, go back the way you came up.

If you do decide to take the steep descent, called the Allerdale Ramble, relief comes on reaching tiny Carlside Tarn on the grass plateau at the base of Carl Side. There is then a short climb to Carl Side at 2420ft (738m).

From here on, the path down is a narrow well-worn concave shape, averaging 1:4 with the ground falling away disturbingly on your left. It becomes a bit of a scramble again passing through the outcrops of White Stones and Doups to the corner of a wood, where it turns right to meet the back road in Millbeck. Continue onto the road proper between Millbeck Farm and The Cottage **C**; in the latter you can get tea and cakes in what is probably one of the smallest cottage gardens in England.

Millbeck, now a quiet hamlet of a few cottages, was in the early 19th century a bustling little village with a corn mill as well as a woollen mill that employed 100 people making blankets for export to North America and the Caribbean. To complete the circle, there is now a 2-mile (3.2km) walk along the road through Applethwaite back to the car park, more a lane than a road, passing several interesting properties and for much of the way lined with oaks. The last mile (1.6km) is an ascent of some 600ft (183m). ●

The south end of Allerdale Ramble from Skiddaw

Langdale Pikes

Start	New Dungeon Ghyll Hotel
Distance	9 miles (14.5km)
Approximate time	6½ hours
Parking	National Trust car park by New Dungeon Ghyll Hotel
Refreshments	New and Old Dungeon Ghyll hotels
Ordnance Survey maps	Landranger 90 (Penrith, Keswick & Ambleside), Outdoor Leisure 6 (The English Lakes – South Western area)

The Langdale Pikes are a much admired sight by motorists driving up the east side of Windermere towards Ambleside or when seen across Blea Tarn, one of the classic Lakeland scenes reproduced in countless books and calendars. Although only a little over 2000ft (610m) in height, their stark, crenellated tops give them the appearance of little Alps, compared with the gentler flat- or round-topped fells around them. When approaching them through the Great Langdale valley, they suddenly rise up ahead almost vertically from the valley floor to form a line of great crags, buttresses and screes. There are many tracks to their summits – some are hard scrambles, others hard walks. There are no easy options. To gain 2000ft (610m) in little over a ¹/₂-mile (800m), in places using hands and feet to negotiate rock outcrops, is to approach the borderline between walking and climbing. This route up to and along the length of the Pikes takes the walker to the finest viewpoints for scanning the heart of the volcanic mountain region of south-west Lakeland. It is a strenuous exercise, which should be kept for fine, dry weather and should not be attempted in bad weather unless you are an experienced walker able to navigate by using a compass.

Start at the National Trust car park by the New Dungeon Ghyll Hotel and take the hillside path to the Old Dungeon Ghyll Hotel, following the signed path to Dungeon Ghyll and Mickleden, a pleasant ³/₄-mile (1.2km) stroll. Alternatively, it is possible to start at the Old Dungeon Ghyll Hotel **Ⓐ**, where there is also a National Trust car park.

Round the back of the Old Dungeon Ghyll Hotel, go through a gate onto a wide, stony road past Middle Fell Farm. On your right, the towering rock faces of Raven Crag and White Crag overlook the road, while to your left is the broad flood-plain of Great Langdale Beck, soon to become Mickleden Beck. After two gates the road becomes a rough track along the floor of Mickleden, a beautiful, shallow U-shaped glacial valley, running between Crinkle Crags and Bow Fell in the south-west and the distinctive and isolated, pepperpot-shaped Pike of Stickle to the north-east, flanked by a line of lesser crags. It is a marvellous short stretch into the very heart of the Borrowdale volcanic group. Dozens of mountain streams on both sides cascade down through rock and scree like tinsel streamers. For a time the black rock walls of Rosset Crag and Black Crags appear to block the end of the valley with no apparent way to walk out. But, as the beck and track curve to the right, the thin white line of Stake Gill, falling down from Langdale Combe, appears ahead and, just discernible, a path zigzagging beside it. While walking below the scree slopes of Pike of Stickle, consider that 5000 years ago the tops of those screes formed one of the most productive axe factories in the land. High up on the unstable slopes our neolithic ancestors hacked away at flint-like rock to make axe-heads, which were traded all over Britain. At the head of the valley the ground is covered with dozens of moraines, piles of debris dumped by the last retreating glacier.

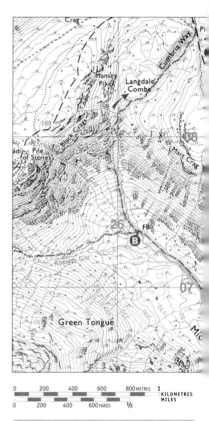

The time to start climbing comes after passing a stone-walled sheepfold, then cross a wooden bridge Ⓑ over the beck, where it is joined by Stake Gill. From the bridge a path turns up to the right through bracken alongside Stake Gill for 800ft (244m), with hairpin bends keeping the gradient comfortable to the top of Langdale Combe. It is a well-engineered path with, in many sections, large stone cobbles placed at the right angle and with convenient rises for steady walking. Looking back, there is always the magnificent view down Mickleden, and ahead one is almost level with the summit of Pike of Stickle, even though it is still 1 mile (1.6km) away. This steep rock path eventually comes out onto a gentler

gradient to wander between another area of moraine humps to reach the cairn and little tarn at the head of Stake Pass. Just before reaching them, turn sharp right ⒸΟΡΤ and, ignoring the path soon going off left up to High Raise, make for the solitary lump of Pike of Stickle. There is a path, but it is a mishmash of grass, peat and stones and takes in a few dog-legs on the way. This is squidgy walking as much of the ground is boggy, but with an eye on the Pike it is impossible to get lost. There is a bit of a climb to the base of the summit, some 600ft (183m) in fact, but there the walking becomes easier with a stony path running through grass, first downhill across the top of Dungeon Ghyll ⒹΟΒ and then up to Harrison Stickle and round the back of Pavey Ark. For those with a mind for a bit of scrambling there are plenty of ways up to the summits of Pike of Stickle and Harrison Stickle, and a grass slope leads onto the top of the great

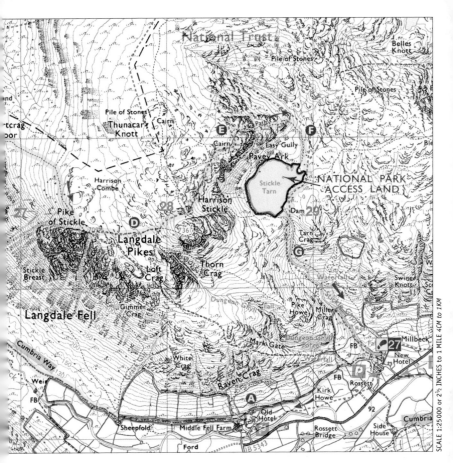

SCALE 1:25000 or 2½ INCHES to 1 MILE 4CM to 1KM

cliff of Pavey Ark. All three tops are grandstands for far-reaching views over the fells and peaks to the south and west.

Weather permitting, one looks down on the fresh green of Mickleden and the Great Langdale valley, which in autumn is clothed in purple heather. Lifting the eyes, one may be able to see places as far off as Windermere and even Morecambe Bay. Along this path there are some cairns to guide you, but care must be taken when leaving the one on Pavey Ark because the right of way, marked on the map as curving round its outlying north crags, no longer exists as a path. Instead, turn right **E** on a grass shoulder and go down a fairly steep gully, part grass, part rock, marked 'Path' on the map but known as North Rake Gully, and at the bottom cross over Bright Beck **F** which is quite shallow, with plenty of natural stepping-stones. On

the other side, follow a well-trodden way round Stickle Tarn to the dam. To connect with the steep track down to New Dungeon Ghyll Hotel, cross over to the far side of Stickle Ghyll, using a row of stones across the overflow. The descent starts on the right side of the gill, which is virtually an intermittent waterfall all the way down. Below Tarn Crag it drops into a pool, where you need to cross back **G** to the left bank by walking across the rim of the next waterfall. Near the bottom of the descent, cross a wooden bridge back onto the right-hand side again, before arriving on the level beside the hotel. This steep track has in parts been made up with stone cobbles, but there are short sections where hands as well as feet are needed to negotiate outcrops. It can be a knee-jarring trip, but the view into Great Langdale is quite stunning.

LANGDALE PIKES ● 85

Scafell Pike

Start	Wasdale Head
Distance	8 miles (12.9km)
Approximate time	7 hours
Parking	Wasdale Head car park
Refreshments	Inn at Wasdale Head
Ordnance Survey maps	Landranger 89 (West Cumbria), Outdoor Leisure 6 (The English Lakes – South Western area)

Scafell Pike, at 3210ft (978m), is the highest mountain in England, which for many people is sufficient reason for wanting to climb it. The mountain is a bleak, rocky wilderness, virtually hidden in surrounding crags, whose naked rock walls are surmounted by sharp pinnacles. It is these towering crags that create the most dramatic effect on the approach to the final assault. The routes both up and down have in many places been well made up, and most precipitous sections are stepped, but along the Corridor Route there are ledges above sheer drops and some exposed scrambles. In perfect weather, incomparable views in all directions reward you for the hard work of getting to the summit, but such occasions are few; even in the height of summer mist or cloud can bring visibility down to yards rather than miles. After heavy rain the gills and becks will be in spate, so walkers should be prepared to get wet feet. On no account should this walk be attempted in winter or bad weather unless you are experienced in fellwalking in such conditions and able to use a compass.

From Wasdale Head, walk south down the road past the former school building and turn through the left of two gates **Ⓐ** signposted 'Sca Fell'. Cross a field and a wooden bridge over Lingmell Beck, then turn right and start up the fellside, following a clear track round the foot of Lingmell and alongside the ravine carrying Lingmell Gill. Ahead will be seen the concave slope of Brown Tongue with a path running up its centre line. Before reaching the Tongue, the wide, fast-flowing gill has to be crossed **Ⓑ**. This can

normally be done boulder-to-boulder without getting wet, but if it is in spate some wading will be involved. The old path up the backbone of Brown Tongue has been replaced by a new one, extremely well made with cobbles and rock steps along its side, following a steep gradient. This takes you up to Hollow Stones, at the beginning of which the track splits **Ⓒ**.

Take the left-hand track, which although no longer made up is initially lined on both sides with small boulders.

Hollow Stones is an area of huge boulders, some as big as garden sheds, between which you must wander. The wandering is determined by numerous cairns, and in season you can enjoy the blueberries that carpet the ground. The peculiar ascent roller-coasts over numerous ridges, and as height is gained Scafell Crag and Symonds Knott lower, dark and threatening over one's left shoulder, with their ridges lined by sharp pinnacles. Ahead, rising up some 600ft (183m) are the equally intimidating black walls of Pikes Crag and Pulpit Rock. The way is cairned up to Lingmell Col, where the track again divides. To the left is the way down to the Corridor Route, but turning right **D** takes you up to Scafell Pike. It is an easily found, well-worn track over rock with a few Z-bends and soon leaves all vegetation behind. Before long, in clear

The Corridor Route from Scafell Pike over Stand Crag

weather, you will see the top looking like a mushroom cap. It is the largest cairn in the land, walled round at its base, with a dome of stones. This final climb rises 600ft (180m) in about 800 yds (730m). Three paths reach the summit from different directions so it is wise to note the view behind you on the ascent to be sure that you take the same route down.

From the summit it is possible, when the air is clear, to count over 100 pikes and tops breaking the horizon and many more below them. Between east and south-east there lie Windermere and the Pennines far beyond; to the north Derwent Water shows up below Skiddaw, and on the best of days you will see across the Solway Firth to Scotland; in the south the Furness area and Duddon estuary are in sight. Not the least of the views is that across the Irish Sea to the Isle of Man. Even when visibility is limited there is plenty of drama in the nearby massifs of Crinkle Crags, Ill Crag, Broad Crag, Great Gable and the desolate top of Sca Fell. Coming off the summit, return to the cairn on Lingmell Col, where the track divides, and take the steep right-hand track towards the head of Piers Gill **E**. At times it is necessary to clamber through narrow gaps between rocks but there is nothing difficult until Piers Gill, which roars down a deep chasm below Lingmell Crag before taking a right angle turn down into the head of Wasdale. The walker is now confronted with a bad step or ledge little more than 2ft (0.6m) wide with vertical rock on one side and the void of the chasm on the other.

After crossing this narrow ledge, the next feature on the track is the ford at the top of Middleboot Knotts, a tiny, marshy plateau set amidst crags. Continue down-hill onto the next little plateau, Criscliffe Knotts, from where there is a glorious long view across the top of Wasdale Head to Styhead Tarn and on into Borrowdale, across Derwent Water to Keswick and

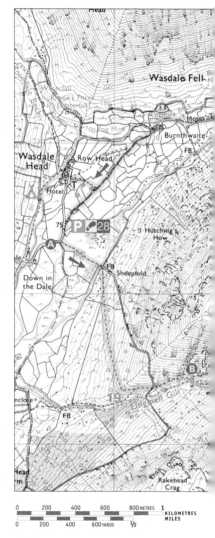

finally Skiddaw. In the immediate fore-ground is the bulk of Great Gable, and climbers may be visible on the famous traverse halfway up its smooth-looking side. Next come another ford **F** and the top of a small ravine carrying a tributary of Greta Gill. There is a clamber down into it, and then a scramble, which could be called a beginner's rock climb: footholds and handholds straight up a rock-face about as high as a two-storey house. You are then on Stand Crag, from where the track makes a high-level traverse of the head of Wasdale, which now opens up below, Great Gable standing full height

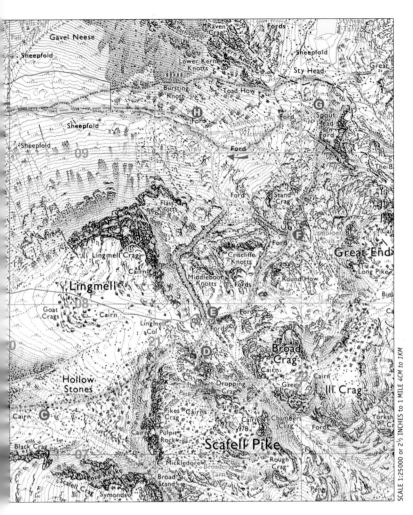

SCALE 1:25000 or 2½ INCHES to 1 MILE 4CM to 1KM

from head to foot before you. Labelled the Corridor Route, the track starts going down behind crags and outcrops to Spout Head Ford, below a waterfall into Skew Gill. From here you can look down on the last leg home along the floor of Wasdale, or by the straight path faintly visible on the lower slope of Great Gable.

To reach the former way, look out for a small cairn beyond Spout Head Ford. Just before reaching it, go down a rough-and-ready path on the left **G**, which leads onto a pony trail that takes a serpentine route down to the valley floor. Eventually, it ends up in the cleft between Piers Gill and Spouthead Gill, where they join to become Lingmell Beck. Where the map says 'Ford' **H**, you will have to wade if the waters are in spate. After crossing, keep alongside Lingmell Beck all the way to Gable Beck and then via Moses Trod to Burnthwaite Farm and on past the church into Wasdale Head village. However, if all the gills and becks are in full flood it might be better to take the path along the side of Great Gable. In this case, carry on past the cairn near Spout Head Ford, climb to Sty Head and then veer left to pass across the end of the track down from Great Gable's summit and along the path that slopes gently down the fellside all the way to Moses Trod. The church near the end of the walk is the smallest in the Lake District, and Wast Water is the deepest lake, complementing Scafell Pike, the highest mountain. ●

Further Information

The National Parks and Countryside Recreation

Ten National Parks were created in England and Wales as a result of an Act of Parliament in 1949. In addition to these, there are numerous specially designated Areas of Outstanding Natural Beauty, Country and Regional Parks, Sites of Special Scientific Interest and picnic areas scattered throughout England, Wales and Scotland, all of which share the twin aims of preservation of the countryside and public accessibility and enjoyment.

John Dower, whose report in 1945 created their framework, defined a National Park as 'an extensive area of beautiful and relatively wild country in which, for the nation's benefit and by appropriate national decision and action, (a) the characteristic landscape beauty is strictly preserved, (b) access and facilities for public open-air enjoyment are amply provided, (c) wildlife and buildings and places of architectural and historic interest are suitably protected, while (d) established farming use is effectively maintained'.

Proposals for the creation of areas of protected countryside were first made before World War I, but nothing was done. The growing demand for access to open country and the reluctance of landowners – particularly those who owned large expanses of uncultivated moorland – to grant it led to a number of ugly incidents, in particular the mass trespass in the Peak District in 1932, when ramblers and gamekeepers came to blows and some trespassers received stiff prison sentences.

It was after World War II that calls for countryside conservation and access came to fruition in parliament. The National Parks and Countryside Act of 1949 provided for the designation and preservation of areas both of great scenic beauty and of particular wildlife and scientific interest throughout Britain. More specifically it provided for the creation of National Parks in England and Wales. Scotland was excluded because, with greater areas of open space and a smaller population, there were fewer pressures on the Scottish countryside.

A National Parks Commission, a forerunner of the Countryside Commission, was set up, and over the next eight years ten areas were designated as parks; seven in England (Northumberland, Lake District, North York Moors, Yorkshire Dales, Peak District, Exmoor and Dartmoor) and three in Wales (Snowdonia, Brecon Beacons and Pembrokeshire Coast). In 1989 the Norfolk and Suffolk Broads were added to the list. At the same time the Commission was also given the responsibility for designating other smaller areas of high recreational and scenic qualities (Areas of Outstanding Natural Beauty), plus the power to propose and develop long-distance footpaths, now called National Trails.

The authorities who administer the individual National Parks have the very difficult task of reconciling the interests of the people who live and earn their living within them with those of visitors. National Parks are not living museums

Eel Tarn and the Eskdale Fells above Boot

and there is pressure to exploit the resources of the area, through more intensive farming, or through increased quarrying and forestry, extraction of minerals or the construction of reservoirs.

In the end it all comes down to a question of balance – between conservation and 'sensitive development'. On the one hand there is a responsibility to preserve the natural beauty of the National Parks and to promote their enjoyment by the public, and on the other, the needs and well-being of the people living and working in them have to be borne in mind.

 ## The National Trust

Anyone who likes visiting places of natural beauty and/or historic interest has cause to be grateful to the National Trust. Without it, many such places would probably have vanished by now.

It was in response to the pressures on the countryside posed by the relentless march of Victorian industrialisation that the trust was set up in 1895. Its founders, inspired by the common goals of protecting and conserving Britain's national heritage and widening public access to it, were Sir Robert Hunter, Octavia Hill and Canon Rawnsley: respectively a solicitor, a social reformer and a clergyman. The latter was particularly influential. As a canon of Carlisle Cathedral and vicar of Crosthwaite (near Keswick), he was concerned about threats to the Lake District and had already been active in protecting footpaths and promoting public access to open countryside. After the flooding of Thirlmere in 1879 to create a large reservoir, he became increasingly convinced that the only effective way to guarantee protection was outright ownership of land.

The purpose of the National Trust is to preserve areas of natural beauty and sites of historic interest by acquisition, holding them in trust for the nation and making them available for public access and enjoyment. Some of its properties have

been acquired through purchase, but many have been donated. Nowadays it is not only one of the biggest landowners in the country, but also one of the most active conservation charities, protecting 581,113 acres (253,176 ha) of land, including 555 miles (892km) of coastline, and over 300 historic properties in England, Wales and Northern Ireland. (There is a separate National Trust for Scotland, which was set up in 1931.)

Furthermore, once a piece of land has come under National Trust ownership, it is difficult for its status to be altered. As a result of parliamentary legislation in 1907, the Trust was given the right to declare its property inalienable, so ensuring that in any subsequent dispute it can appeal directly to parliament.

As it works towards its dual aims of conserving areas of attractive countryside and encouraging greater public access (not easy to reconcile in this age of mass tourism), the Trust provides an excellent service for walkers by creating new concessionary paths and waymarked trails, maintaining stiles and footbridges and combating the ever-increasing problem of footpath erosion.

For details of membership, contact the National Trust at the address on page 95.

 ## The Ramblers' Association

No organisation works more actively to protect and extend the rights and interests of walkers in the countryside than the Ramblers' Association. Its aims are clear: to foster a greater knowledge, love and care of the countryside; to assist in the protection and enhancement of public rights of way and areas of natural beauty; to work for greater public access to the countryside; and to encourage more people to take up rambling as a healthy, recreational leisure activity.

It was founded in 1935 when, following the setting up of a National Council of Ramblers' Federations in 1931, a number of federations earlier formed in London, Manchester, the Midlands and elsewhere came together to create a more effective pressure group, to deal with such problems as the disappearance and obstruction of footpaths, the prevention of access to open mountain and moorland and increasing hostility from landowners. This was the era of the mass trespasses, when there were sometimes violent confrontations between ramblers and gamekeepers, especially on the moorlands of the Peak District.

Since then the Ramblers' Association has played an influential role in preserving and developing the national footpath network, supporting the creation of national parks and encouraging the designation and way-marking of long-distance routes.

Our freedom to walk in the countryside is precarious and requires constant vigilance. As well as the perennial problems of foot-paths being illegally obstructed, disappear-ing through lack of use or extinguished by housing or road construction, new dangers can spring up at any time.

It is to meet such problems and dangers that the Ramblers' Association exists and represents the interests of all walkers. The address to write to for information on the Ramblers' Association and how to become a member is given on page 95.

 ## Walkers and the Law

The average walker in a national park or other popular walking area, armed with the appropriate Ordnance Survey map, reinforced perhaps by a guidebook giving detailed walking instructions, is unlikely to run into legal difficulties, but it is useful to know something about the law relating to public rights of way. The right to walk over certain parts of the countryside has developed over a long period, and how such rights came into being is a complex subject, too lengthy to be discussed here. The following comments are intended simply as a helpful guide, backed up by the Countryside Access Charter, a concise summary of walkers' rights and obligations drawn up by the Countryside Commission.

Basically there are two main kinds of public rights of way: footpaths (for walkers only) and bridleways (for walkers,

riders on horseback and pedal cyclists). Footpaths and bridleways are shown by broken green lines on Ordnance Survey Pathfinder and Outdoor Leisure maps and broken red lines on Landranger maps. There is also a third category, called byways: chiefly broad tracks (green lanes) or farm roads, which walkers, riders and cyclists have to share, usually only occasionally, with motor vehicles. Many of these public paths have been in existence for hundreds of years and some even originated as prehistoric trackways and have been in constant use for well over 2000 years. Ways known as RUPPs (roads used as public paths) still appear on some maps. The legal definition of such byways is ambiguous and they are gradually being reclassified as footpaths, bridleways or byways.

The term 'right of way' means exactly what it says. It gives right of passage over what, in the vast majority of cases, is private land, and you are required to keep to the line of the path and not stray on to the land on either side. If you inadvert-ently wander off the right of way – either because of faulty map-reading or because the route is not clearly indicated on the ground – you are technically trespassing and the wisest course is to ask the nearest available person (farmer or fellow walker) to direct you back to the correct route. There are stories about unpleasant con-frontations between walkers and farmers at times, but in general most farmers are co-operative when responding to a genuine and polite request for assistance in route-finding.

Obstructions can sometimes be a problem and probably the most common of these is where a path across a field has been ploughed up. It is legal for a farmer to plough up a path provided that he restores it within two weeks, barring exceptionally bad weather. This does not always happen and here the walker is presented with a dilemma: to follow the line of the path, even if this inevitably means treading on crops, or to walk around the edge of the field. The latter course of action often seems the best but

Countryside Access Charter

Your rights of way are:

- public footpaths – on foot only. Sometimes waymarked in yellow
- bridleways – on foot, horseback and pedal cycle. Sometimes waymarked in blue
- byways (usually old roads), most 'roads used as public paths' and, of course, public roads – all traffic has the right of way

Use maps, signs and waymarks to check rights of way. Ordnance Survey Pathfinder and Landranger maps show most public rights of way

On rights of way you can:

- take a pram, pushchair or wheelchair if practicable
- take a dog (on a lead or under close control)
- take a short route round an illegal obstruction or remove it sufficiently to get past

You have a right to go for recreation to:

- public parks and open spaces – on foot
- most commons near older towns and cities – on foot and sometimes on horseback
- private land where the owner has a formal agreement with the local authority

In addition you can use the following by local or established custom or consent, but ask for advice if you are unsure:

- many areas of open country, such as moorland, fell and coastal areas, especially those in the care of the National Trust, and some commons
- some woods and forests, especially those owned by the Forestry Commission
- country parks and picnic sites
- most beaches
- canal towpaths
- some private paths and tracks Consent sometimes extends to horse-riding and cycling

For your information:

- county councils and London boroughs maintain and record rights of way, and register commons
- obstructions, dangerous animals, harassment and misleading signs on rights of way are illegal and you should report them to the county council
- paths across fields can be ploughed, but must normally be reinstated within two weeks
- landowners can require you to leave land to which you have no right of access
- motor vehicles are normally permitted only on roads, byways and some 'roads used as public paths'

this means that you would be trespassing and not keeping to the exact line of the path. In the case of other obstructions which may block a path (illegal fences and locked gates etc), common sense has to be used in order to negotiate them by the easiest method – detour or removal. You should only ever remove as much as is necessary to get through, and if you can easily go round the obstruction without causing any damage, then you should do so. If you have any problems negotiating rights of way, you should report the matter to the rights of way department of the relevant council, which will take action with the landowner concerned.

Apart from rights of way enshrined by law, there are a number of other paths

available to walkers. Permissive or concessionary paths have been created where a landowner has given permission for the public to use a particular route across his land. The main problem with these is that, as they have been granted as a concession, there is no legal right to use them and therefore they can be extinguished at any time. In practice, many of these concessionary routes have been established on land owned either by large public bodies such as the Forestry Commission, or by a private one, such as the National Trust, and as these mainly encourage walkers to use their paths, they are unlikely to be closed unless a change of ownership occurs.

Walkers also have free access to

country parks (except where requested to keep away from certain areas for ecological reasons, eg. wildlife protection, woodland regeneration, safeguarding of rare plants etc), canal towpaths and most beaches. By custom, though not by right, you are generally free to walk across the open and uncultivated higher land of mountain, moorland and fell, but this varies from area to area and from one season to another – grouse moors, for example, will be out of bounds during the breeding and shooting seasons and some open areas are used as Ministry of Defence firing ranges, for which reason access will be restricted. In some areas the situation has been clarified as a result of 'access agreements' between the landowners and either the county council or the national park authority, which clearly define when and where you can walk over such open country.

Ullswater from Hallin Fell

 ### Safety on the Hills

The hills, mountains and moorlands of Britain, though of modest height compared with those in many other countries, need to be treated with respect. Friendly and inviting in good weather, they can quickly be transformed into wet, misty, windswept and potentially dangerous areas of wilderness in bad weather. Even on an outwardly fine and settled summer day, conditions can rapidly deteriorate at high altitudes and, in winter, even more so.

Therefore it is advisable to always take both warm and waterproof clothing, sufficient nourishing food, a hot drink, first-aid kit, torch and whistle. Wear suitable footwear, such as strong walking-boots or shoes that give a good grip over rocky terrain and on slippery slopes. Try to obtain a local weather forecast and bear it in mind before you start. Do not be afraid to abandon your proposed route and return to your starting point in the event of a sudden and unexpected deterioration in the weather. Do not go alone and allow enough time to finish the walk well before nightfall.

Most of the walks described in this book do not venture into remote wilderness areas and will be safe to do, given due care and respect, at any time of year in all but the most unreasonable weather. Indeed, a crisp, fine winter day often provides perfect walking conditions, with firm ground underfoot and a clarity that is not possible to achieve in the other seasons of the year. A few walks, however, are suitable only for reasonably fit and experienced hill walkers able to use a compass and should definitely not be tackled by anyone else during the winter months or in bad weather, especially high winds and mist. These are indicated in the general description that precedes each of the walks.

 ### Useful Organisations

Council for National Parks
246 Lavender Hill, London SW11 1LJ.
Tel. 020 7924 4077

Council for the Protection of Rural England
25 Buckingham Palace Road, London SW1W 0PP.
Tel. 020 7976 6433

Countryside Agency
John Dower House, Crescent Place, Cheltenham, Gloucestershire GL50 3RA.
Tel. 01242 521381

Cumbria Tourist Board
Ashleigh, Holly Road, Windermere, Cumbria LA23 2AQ.
Tel. 015394 44444

Forestry Commission
Information Dept, 231 Corstorphine Road,
Edinburgh EH12 7AT.
Tel. 0131 334 0303

Friends of the Lake District
Murley Moss, Oxenholme Road,
Kendal, Cumbria LA9 7SS.
Tel. 01539 720788

Lake District National Park Authority
information centres (*not open all year*):
*Ambleside: 01539 432729
*Bowness Bay: 015394 42895
*Broughton-in-Furness: 01229 716115
*Coniston: 015394 41533
*Glenridding: 017684 82414
*Grasmere: 015394 35245
*Hawkshead: 015394 36525
Keswick: 017687 72645
*Pooley Bridge: 017684 86530
*Seatoller: 017687 77294
*Waterhead: 015394 32729

Lake District National Park
Visitor Centre
Brockhole, Windermere, Cumbria LA23 1LJ.
Tel. 015394 46601

Long Distance Walkers' Association
21 Upcroft, Windsor, Berkshire SL4 3NH.
Tel. 01753 866685

National Trust
Membership and general enquiries:
PO Box 39, Bromley, Kent BR1 3XL.
Tel. 020 8315 1111
North-west regional office:
The Hollens, Grasmere,
Ambleside, Cumbria LA22 9QZ.
Tel. 015394 35599

Ordnance Survey
Romsey Road, Maybush,
Southampton SO16 4GU.
Tel. 08456 05 05 05 (Lo-call)

Ramblers' Association
2nd Floor, Camelford House,
87–90 Albert Embankment,
London SE1 7TW.
Tel. 020 7339 8500

Ravenglass and Eskdale Railway
Ravenglass, Cumbria CA18 1SW.
Tel. 01229 717278

Youth Hostels Association
Trevelyan House, 8 St Stephen's Hill,
St Albans, Hertfordshire AL1 2DY.
Tel. 01727 855215

Ordnance Survey Maps of the Lake District

The Lake District is covered by Ordnance
Survey 1:50 000 (1$\frac{1}{4}$ inches to 1 mile or
2cm to 1km) scale Landranger map sheets
89, 90, 96 and 97). These all-purpose
maps are packed with information to help
you explore the area. Viewpoints, picnic
sites, places of interest and caravan and
camping sites are shown, as well as public
rights of way information such as footpaths and bridleways.

To examine the Lake District in more
detail, and especially if you are planning
walks, Ordnance Survey Outdoor Leisure
maps at 1:25 000 (2$\frac{1}{2}$ inches to 1 mile or
4cm to 1km) scale are ideal. Four such
maps cover the main Lake District
National Park:

Sheet 4 – The English Lakes –
North Western area
Sheet 5 – The English Lakes –
North Eastern area
Sheet 6 – The English Lakes –
South Western area
Sheet 7 – The English Lakes –
South Eastern area

The Lake District area is also covered by
Ordnance Survey Touring map number 3,
at 1 inch to 1 mile (approx. 2.5cm to
1.6km) scale, which includes useful guide
information on the reverse.

To get to the Lake District, use the
Ordnance Survey Great Britain Route-
planner Travelmaster map number 1 at
1:625 000 (1 inch to 10 miles or 1cm to
6.25km) scale or Travelmaster map 5
(Northern England) at 1:250 000 (1 inch to
4 miles or 1cm to 2.5km) scale.

Ordnance Survey maps and guides are
available from most booksellers, stationers
and newsagents.

Index

Entries in *italic type* refer to illustrations